Does God not Exist?

The Rajabali - Barker Debate (2003)

By: Truth Seeker

Edited by: Tawheed Institute Australia

First Edition (2025)

Tawheed Institute Australia Ltd.
Sydney, Australia
www.tawheed.com.au

All rights reserved © 2025
First Edition 1446/2025

Based on the debate between Hassanain Rajabali and Dan Barker which took place in Queens, NY at the Islamic Institute of New York on January 5th, 2003.

Published by Tawheed Institute Australia Ltd.
Sydney, Australia
www.tawheed.com.au

"Some people say that the absence of evidence is not the evidence of absence. But I disagree. If something is truly not existent, then the only evidence we can possibly have for its non-existence would be the absence of evidence for its existence. The absence of evidence is not proof, but it is certainly evidence. If god is obvious, and if god does exist, if there is evidence for it, then why are we having this debate?"
(Dan Barker)

"If a person lacks the understanding to grasp something, it is perfectly reasonable for them to say, 'I don't know.' But that uncertainty should not lead to denial. Just because you haven't found evidence yet doesn't mean it doesn't exist. Instead, that uncertainty should inspire further search and inquiry—especially when there is already ample evidence around us. To say 'I don't know' is an honest position. But to jump from 'I haven't seen it' to 'It does not exist' is not a conclusion based on reason—it's a premature rejection of the pursuit of truth."
(Hassanain Rajabali)

Contents

Foreword vi

The Debaters xi

Preface by the Author 1

Introduction 3

Prologue 8

The Debate Transcript 11

    Opening Statements By Dan Barker 11
    Rebuttal By Hassanain Rajabali 20
    Reply By Dan Barker 24
    Opening Statements by Hassanain Rajabali 26
    Rebuttal by Dan Barker 35
    Reply by Hassanain Rajabali 40
    Questions from the Audience 42
    Closing Statements by Dan Barker 61
    Closing Statements by Hassanain Rajabali 63

Brief Commentary 67

    Opening Arguments 67
    Hassanain Rajabali's Rebuttal 69
    Dan Barker's Rebuttal 72
    Q&A Session 76

Detail Review of Key Arguments 81

    The Problem of Evil 81
    Can God Be Both All-Merciful and All-Just? 84
    Can God's Existence Be Tested? 86
    An Essay on The Principle Falsifiability 88
    Morality Without God? 94
    The Argument from the Universe 98
    The "God of the Gaps" Argument 103
    God: Beyond Frame of Reference 106
    The 'Married Bachelor' Analogy 110
    Barker's "One Less God Argument" 112
    Absence of Evidence or Evidence of Absence? 115
    Characterization of the Qur'an 119

Critique of Richard Carrier's Review 123

    Introduction 123
    Argument from the Universe: 124
    Argument from Absolute Morality 141
    The "Trial Defense" and the Argument from Evil 143
    Shoring up Agnosticism 146
    Pitching Balls for the Home Team 150

Epilogue 157

Foreword

In the name of God, the Most Gracious, the Most Merciful.

The question of God's existence remains one of the most enduring and fiercely debated subjects in human thought. For centuries, it has commanded the attention of philosophers, theologians, scientists, poets, and the everyday seeker of truth. While many philosophical and theological arguments have been advanced in both affirmation and denial of God's existence, it is perhaps in the crucible of live debate—where worldviews collide in real time—that such questions acquire not only logical depth but human immediacy.

The present work, Does God Not Exist?, takes as its foundation one such rare and riveting encounter: the public debate between Dan Barker, a former evangelical minister turned atheist and spokesperson for secular humanism, and Hassanain Rajabali, a prominent Islamic scholar and theist grounded in classical metaphysics. What makes this debate particularly compelling is not only the contrasting positions of its participants, but the wide philosophical terrain they traverse—from cosmology and evolution to morality, the problem of evil, and the limits of human reason.

But this book is not simply a transcript or commentary. It is a layered intellectual project. It seeks to present the debate in its raw form, review its arguments in a balanced and structured manner, include a widely-read third-party critique by philosopher and historian Richard Carrier, and then offer a point-by-point assessment of that critique, testing its fairness, rigor, and underlying assumptions. In so doing, the book becomes more than just a record of a single event—it becomes a microcosm of the larger discourse on belief and unbelief in the modern world.

The Significance of the Title: "Does God Not Exist?"

The very title of the debate—Does God Not Exist?—is itself a strategic inversion of the standard formulation. Traditionally, the burden of proof is placed on the theist to demonstrate the existence of God: Does God exist? This formulation invites the atheist to adopt a default position of non-belief until sufficient evidence is provided. Inverting the title to Does God not Exist? subtly shifts the terrain, placing a more active burden of defense on the atheist to justify the non-existence of God. While this may appear to be a minor linguistic turn, it has important philosophical and rhetorical implications, especially in a debate format.

The book opens with a prologue that explores this strategic dimension of the debate and how it shaped the tone, expectations, and direction of the arguments presented. This lens is particularly important because debates are not just intellectual contests; they are also performative events, where framing and strategy can influence perception as much as substance.

Presenting the Debate Itself:

The heart of the book is, of course, the transcript of the debate itself. This is more than a routine transcription; it has been formatted to preserve the flow and spontaneity of live speech, while also clarifying and structuring the arguments for ease of reference. The transcript captures not only what was said, but the style, tone, and emotional register of each debater. Rajabali's impassioned appeals to divine justice and purpose are balanced against Barker's cool and rationalist emphasis on humanism and empiricism. The audience reactions—whether laughter, applause, or thoughtful silence—also offer insight into the cultural context and rhetorical effectiveness of each speaker.

Yet, the transcript alone does not answer the deep philosophical questions at stake. And this is where the second half of the book comes in.

A Detailed Review Without Scores:

Following the transcript is a structured review of the debate.

Importantly, this is done without assigning scores or winners, because the goal is not to reduce the discussion to a point-based system, but to unpack the philosophical substance of each argument. Each major theme is treated as a self-contained section: the cosmological arguments, the problem of evil, the argument from design, the argument from morality, and so on.

The review considers what each speaker said, how their arguments relate to existing philosophical literature, and whether they addressed each other's positions effectively. It is a blend of descriptive analysis and gentle critique, intended to give the reader a clear sense of where the arguments were strong, where they faltered, and what was left unsaid.

This part of the book is designed to serve both specialist and generalist readers. Philosophers will appreciate the references to metaphysical traditions, logical structure, and epistemic standards. Lay readers will benefit from the clarity and fairness of the summaries, which do not presume prior knowledge but invite further exploration.

Critique of Richard Carrier's Review:

One of the unique features of this book is a thorough critique of Richard Carrier's review. Carrier, an outspoken atheist scholar with a background in history and philosophy attended the debate and subsequently published a widely circulated critique that accused Rajabali of emotional manipulation, fallacious reasoning, and theological inconsistency. He also pointed out missed opportunities on Barker's part, particularly in responding to moral and metaphysical arguments.

This is where the conversation reaches its most reflective level, because it is no longer just about what Rajabali or Barker said, but about how we interpret what they said, and what standards we use to evaluate it.

The critique addresses each of Carrier's points, examining whether he fairly represented Rajabali's arguments, whether his philosophical objections were sound, and whether he overlooked or misinterpreted key parts of the transcript. In some cases, the critique agrees with Carrier—especially where Barker missed opportunities or where certain theological claims were not defended rigorously. But in many cases, it finds that Carrier either misunderstood Rajabali's metaphysical framework, or applied philosophical categories that didn't fit the structure of Islamic theism.

For example, when Carrier accuses Rajabali of fallacious reasoning in his moral argument, the critique shows that what Rajabali was actually presenting was a moral ontology challenge—a question about the grounding of objective moral values—which cannot be dismissed as merely emotional or manipulative. Similarly, where Carrier charges that Rajabali's "Trial Defense" of evil is morally reprehensible, the critique explains how this is based on Islamic theodicy, which sees suffering not as gratuitous but as a means of spiritual growth.

Thus, this section of the book is not merely a counter-attack. It is a demonstration of how philosophical discourse functions: through claim and counter-claim, through interpretation and reinterpretation, and through the continual refining of arguments in the light of critique.

The Broader Significance:

While this book is structured around a single debate, it reaches far beyond it. It explores the epistemology of belief and unbelief, the existential stakes of morality and suffering, and the limits of reason in the face of mystery. It is a book that takes seriously both the strengths of theism and the challenge of atheism, and insists that neither should be caricatured.

It also raises vital cultural and political questions. In a time when religious and secular worldviews are often weaponized against each other, this book models a different kind of engagement: one that is rigorous, respectful, and grounded in mutual accountability. Rajabali and Barker disagreed passionately, but they did not dehumanize each other. This, too, is a lesson worth preserving.

Final Word:

Whether you are a theist or an atheist, a seeker or a skeptic, this book invites you into a higher form of debate—one that values truth over victory, clarity over applause, and understanding over certainty. In presenting not just a debate but its layered reviews and meta-critiques, Does God Not Exist? offers a rare opportunity: to see how philosophical positions are constructed, challenged, and revised in real time and over time.

The hope is not merely to convince you of a particular position, but to inspire you to think more carefully about your own—and to equip you with the tools to engage others with fairness, depth, and courage.

Tawheed Institute Australia Ltd.
April 2025

About the Author:

Truth Seeker is a writer, researcher, and independent thinker committed to exploring the timeless questions of existence, belief, and meaning. With a passion for dialogue and a deep respect for diverse worldviews, *Truth Seeker* aims to bring clarity, depth, and fairness to some of the most contentious debates of our time.

This work, Does God Not Exist?, is not an attempt to preach or convert—it is a sincere effort to examine the arguments, test assumptions, and invite readers into a shared journey of reflection and inquiry. Stepping beyond labels and ideologies, *Truth Seeker* believes that the pursuit of truth begins with honest questions, careful reasoning, and the courage to listen across divides.

The Debaters

Hassanain Rajabali:

Rajabali is a respected public speaker, educator, and community leader whose work bridges science, philosophy, and Islamic ethics. Born in Tanzania and based in Dearborn, Michigan, he brings a rich multicultural perspective to his advocacy for intellectual and spiritual development.

He holds degrees in molecular biology and psychology from the University of Colorado, grounding his interdisciplinary approach to questions of existence, morality, and human purpose. His talks are known for blending scientific insight with theological reasoning, making him a prominent voice in modern Islamic discourse.

Rajabali has addressed global audiences on topics such as belief, ethics, and secularism. Formerly Principal of the Tawheed Institute in New York, he also ran a successful internet company, showcasing his entrepreneurial drive.

He now directs Camp Taha, the first Muslim-owned residential camp in Columbiaville, Michigan, and leads WISE Learning, an initiative promoting character and critical thinking.

Through education and ethical leadership, Hassanain Rajabali continues to inspire diverse audiences to pursue truth, justice, and spiritual growth.

Dan Barker:

Barker is an American author, public speaker, and prominent advocate for atheism and secular humanism. A former evangelical Christian preacher and musician, Barker served in ministry for 19 years before publicly renouncing his faith in 1984. He is the co-president of the Freedom From Religion Foundation (FFRF), one of the largest secular organizations in the United States, dedicated to promoting the constitutional principle of separation between church and state.

Barker is best known for his journey from devout believer to outspoken atheist, chronicled in his widely read book Losing Faith in Faith: From Preacher to Atheist. He has since authored several other works exploring theology, ethics, and the role of religion in public life. A skilled debater, he has participated in numerous public forums challenging religious claims and advocating for reason-based ethics.

Blending personal narrative, philosophical critique, and activism, Dan Barker remains a leading voice in contemporary atheism and secular advocacy.

Preface By The Author

In recent decades, the discourse on the existence or non-existence of God has shifted beyond traditional theological and philosophical domains and into the sphere of modern science, cognitive theory, and probabilistic reasoning. Atheistic arguments today are no longer confined to the classical problem of evil or questions about divine hiddenness. Thinkers such as Victor J. Stenger, Richard Dawkins, and others have introduced a wide range of frameworks that challenge the plausibility of God—not only through philosophical reasoning but through appeals to cosmology, evolutionary biology, neuroscience, and Bayesian probability.

Victor Stenger, in his book *God: The Failed Hypothesis*, argues that if God plays a causal role in the functioning of the universe and in human experience—as theists claim—then we should expect to see some empirical signature of that divine involvement. In the absence of such signatures, he concludes that the universe looks exactly as it would if no God existed. Others, like Richard Dawkins, have popularized the idea that natural selection and random mutation are sufficient to account for the diversity and complexity of life, rendering a divine designer superfluous. More recently, the cognitive science of religion has offered psychological explanations for the emergence of belief in gods, positing that such beliefs arise from evolved cognitive tendencies rather than revealed truths. Philosophers have further argued that theistic explanations are weakened by the availability of naturalistic alternatives, such as the multiverse hypothesis, and have pressed the idea that a good, personal, all-powerful deity is statistically unlikely given the amount of suffering, confusion, and divine silence observed in the world.

I am fully aware of these arguments and their growing influence, especially in academic and popular atheist circles. They have given rise to new forms of skepticism, new styles of atheism, and new rhetorical strategies in public discourse and debates. However, the purpose of this book is not to catalogue or rebut each of these arguments in detail. Instead, this work is focused on a single, yet significant event: a live public debate between Dan Barker and Hassanain Rajabali. This debate, held at the Tawheed Institute in New York, was not a peer-reviewed academic symposium, but a dynamic, spontaneous, and honest exchange of worldviews—a place where ideas were challenged in real time and beliefs were tested in the public square. It was also Dan Barker's first encounter with a Muslim scholar!

While the debate did not explicitly invoke every modern atheistic theory, it nonetheless touched upon many of the underlying issues: the nature of evidence, the definition of reason, the foundations of morality, the plausibility of divine design, and the limits of science. Barker's criticisms of theism mirrored the popular objections of the so-called "New Atheists," while Rajabali's responses echoed the metaphysical, moral, and rational case made by classical and contemporary theists. In many ways, the discussion served as a microcosm of the broader philosophical clash between naturalism and theism.

This book, therefore, is not intended to be a complete theological treatise or an encyclopedic defense of God's existence. It is a close reading and reflection on this singular debate and what it reveals about the strengths, weaknesses, and assumptions of both sides. In presenting a cleaned-up transcript, an internal review of the arguments, and a careful critique of a well-known atheist review of the debate, my goal is to foster deeper thought—not only about the claims themselves but about the methods we use to approach them.

For those seeking rigorous philosophical engagement with cosmological, epistemological, or probabilistic arguments for or against God, there exists a rich and ongoing literature. But for those seeking to understand how these ideas are actually exchanged, defended, and tested in the context of live dialogue, this book offers a unique vantage point. It is in this spirit that I invite readers—both believers and skeptics—to read what follows not merely to win or lose arguments, but to better understand the enduring human quest for truth.

Introduction

In the tumultuous aftermath of the September 11 attacks, the global conversation around religion, belief, and the role of faith in public life took on new urgency and complexity. The dust had not yet fully settled in lower Manhattan when a remarkable and timely debate took place in a quiet neighborhood in Woodside, New York—one that sought not only to answer the age-old question of God's existence but to bridge the growing divide between faith-based and secular worldviews.

On January 5th, 2003, the Islamic Institute of New York became the stage for what would soon be recognized as a memorable intellectual exchange between Dan Barker, a prominent atheist and public advocate for secularism, and Hassanain Rajabali, a Muslim scholar and public speaker known for his articulate defense of theism and Islamic philosophy. The title of the debate was provocative and strategically flipped from its more familiar formulation—"Does God Not Exist?"—thus shifting the usual burden of proof and reframing the entire discussion.

The event was hosted and organized by the Tawheed Institute of New York, an Islamic educational organization whose mission includes fostering interfaith dialogue, critical reflection, and moral consciousness among youth and the wider public. The significance of this debate extended beyond the academic arguments presented: it was a rare opportunity for engagement between diverging worldviews at a time of heightened fear, suspicion, and stereotype-driven hostility. The Institute's vision for this event was rooted in openness, honesty, and mutual respect, emphasizing that meaningful debate need not result in division but can rather become a vehicle for greater understanding.

The event was introduced by Muhammad Jaffer, the Assistant Principal of the Tawheed Institute. In his heartfelt welcome, he set the tone for the evening, reminding the audience that this gathering was part of a broader initiative launched by the Institute after the tragedy of September 11 to create spaces for the sharing of faith, values, and human dignity:

"This is part of a series (of events) that we have done after September 11… a sharing of faith with many groups of people… Though it's an Islamic school, and an Islamic center, we are not going to be biased here with anybody or any group. I guess the main purpose we are here today is to share faith and to get an understanding of each other".

He concluded with a plea that encapsulated the spirit of the gathering: a call to lay aside emotional biases and engage with open minds and hearts. This appeal for intellectual humility and respect resonated through the night and helped guide the exchanges that followed.

The atmosphere was one of tension mixed with curiosity. The debate drew a diverse audience—students, freethinkers, clergy, skeptics, believers, and members of various philosophical and religious communities. Representatives from The Atheists of New York, The Freedom From Religion Foundation, and Columbia University's Muslim Students Association were in attendance. A notable participant in the audience was Dr. Richard Carrier, historian and well-known advocate for naturalism and critical thought, whose later published review would become both a resource and a focal point for further discussion and critique in this book.

Following the welcome, the event commenced with a recitation from the Holy Qur'an by student, invoking verses that reflected divine order, balance, and gratitude, taken from Surah al-Rahmān, which asks again and again: "Which then of the bounties of your Lord will you deny?" The resonance of these verses lingered as the audience settled into their seats for the main event.

The moderator for the evening was Mohamed Athar Lila, a graduate student at Columbia University's School of Journalism, who introduced the speakers and meticulously outlined the format and rules of decorum. His light-hearted manner, combined with his commitment to impartiality, added to the professional conduct of the event. With his own background as a practicing Muslim and an aspiring journalist, he acknowledged his biases upfront and pledged fairness to both participants—a principle he upheld throughout the evening.

The debaters themselves presented a rich contrast in style and background. Dan Barker, a former evangelical Christian preacher turned atheist, had spent nearly two decades in ministry before publicly renouncing his faith. Now a seasoned debater and author of *Losing Faith in Faith: From Preacher to Atheist*, he was the Public Relations Director of the Freedom From Religion Foundation. His opening words affirmed his confidence in reason over faith, evidence over tradition, and secular humanism over divine revelation.

Opposite him stood Hassanain Rajabali, then the Principal of the Tawheed Institute, a seasoned lecturer and articulate thinker who had spoken on Islam at venues such as Columbia University. Trained in business and philosophy, Rajabali's unique blend of rational theism and spiritually grounded ethics had won him a wide following in the Muslim world and beyond. Emigrating from Tanzania and rooted in the American context, he brought a cosmopolitan sensitivity to issues of belief and culture.

The evening was structured with precision: each debater was allotted 20 minutes for opening statements, followed by 10-minute rebuttals, 5-minute replies, closing statements, and a 30-minute audience Q&A, with all questions submitted on paper to maintain decorum. The formal structure lent itself to clarity and allowed both sides to develop their arguments progressively, even as emotions inevitably simmered beneath the surface.

The very title of the debate—"Does God Not Exist?"—was, in many ways, the first point of contention. It subtly but effectively reversed the default setting of religious debate. Traditionally, the onus is on the theist to prove the existence of God. Here, however, the burden fell upon the atheist, challenging Barker to not merely raise doubts or refute inadequate arguments for God but to defend the positive claim that God does not exist. This inversion, though strategically subtle, had a notable psychological effect, shifting the dynamics of the debate and, arguably, placing Barker on the defensive from the outset.

The organizers were fully aware of the sensitivities surrounding this subject, especially in the post-9/11 climate. Faith, culture, and violence had been fused in the public imagination, often in ways that were simplistic and harmful. The Tawheed Institute's efforts to provide a platform where ideas could be exchanged rather than suppressed were a courageous and timely response to these pressures. That this debate occurred just over a year after the attacks gave it a historical weight far beyond its academic subject matter.

Indeed, the thematic undertone of the evening was not merely theological—it was also moral, political, and cultural. Could believers and unbelievers coexist with mutual respect? Could faith be defended rationally, and could atheism offer a compelling account of morality, purpose, and suffering? These questions lingered long after the microphones were turned off.

This book seeks to capture and reflect on the full depth of that encounter. First, it presents a cleaned-up version of the full transcript, ensuring clarity and coherence while preserving the passion and spontaneity of the live exchange. Following the transcript is an independent review that carefully analyzes the arguments and rhetorical strategies of both debaters without attempting to "score" the event. Select portions of Dr. Richard Carrier's published review are then quoted and examined, offering readers a glimpse into a prominent atheist critique of the debate. These excerpts are treated under fair use for the purpose of commentary and analysis. The book concludes with a sustained theistic response to the key claims raised by Carrier, offering counter-arguments, clarifications, and broader reflections on the philosophical assumptions underlying his secular critique.

Through this structure, Does God Not Exist? invites the reader to witness not just a clash of ideologies, but a deeply human effort to grapple with existence itself. Whether one emerges from its pages more convinced of God's necessity or of nature's sufficiency, one will surely come away with a deeper appreciation for the seriousness of the question—and for the importance of confronting it with honesty, civility, and intellectual courage.

Truth Seeker

Prologue

In any formal debate, the framing of the central question is not a mere matter of semantics—it is often a decisive factor in determining the burden of proof and setting the psychological tone for the audience. The title of the debate under review, "Does God Not Exist?", is a subtle but significant deviation from the more commonly posed query: "Does God Exist?" While this might appear to be a minor reversal of phrasing, its implications for the structure of the debate are considerable and worthy of attention.

Traditionally, the question "Does God Exist?" positions the theist as the affirmative party. The burden of proof, in this case, rests with the believer, who must offer compelling arguments or evidence to substantiate the claim of God's existence. The atheist, by contrast, often occupies a more restrained role—challenging the adequacy of the theist's evidence, questioning the coherence of divine attributes, and defending skepticism or non-belief without needing to offer an alternative metaphysical account of existence.

However, by inverting the question to "Does God Not Exist?", the dynamic is quietly but powerfully shifted. The atheist is now implicitly cast in the affirmative role, tasked with demonstrating why God does not exist. This shift in linguistic framing reassigns the burden of proof onto the shoulders of the skeptic, effectively treating theism as the "default" position unless successfully refuted. In doing so, the debate risks misrepresenting the actual epistemic structure of the two positions.

From a philosophical standpoint, this reframing can be problematic. While it is possible to critique the concept of God or highlight contradictions within theological claims, it is notoriously difficult—if not logically impossible—to prove the non-existence of a being whose definition often transcends physical observation, empirical falsifiability, and finite comprehension. The inability to detect or measure something beyond the limits of natural science does not equate to its non-existence, but it also does not justify its existence. Atheists and agnostics often highlight this tension as one of the central reasons for suspending belief rather than asserting confident disbelief.

Thus, the debate title "Does God Not Exist?" subtly but decisively tilts the scale in favor of the theist, placing the atheist in a defensive posture that departs from the usual format. It asks the non-believer to argue a negative—an epistemically awkward position—while giving the theist a rhetorical advantage of presumed belief.

In the actual event, this dynamic played out with nuance. Dan Barker, representing atheism, was tasked with actively defending the position that God does not exist, offering critiques and counterexamples. Hassanain Rajabali, the theistic speaker, benefitted from a posture of spiritual certainty, buttressed by centuries of theological tradition, scriptural authority, and metaphysical reasoning. The burden, consciously or not, appeared to rest more heavily on Barker to disprove rather than on Rajabali to convince.

The choice of title, then, was not merely a linguistic flourish, but a strategic framing device—one that subtly influenced the terms of engagement. Recognizing this effect is essential not only for understanding the debate itself but also for appreciating how rhetoric, language, and framing shape public discourse on matters as profound as the existence of God.

While Barker presented compelling and intelligent arguments against belief in God, he did not fully address the strategic framing of the question "Does God Not Exist?". He operated largely as if the debate were titled "Does God Exist?", focusing on critiques rather than defending a definitive claim of God's non-existence.

In academic terms, we might say that his argumentation was philosophically sound but strategically inattentive to the framing—a missed opportunity that may have subtly affected audience perception and shifted the argumentative burden away from his opponent.

It is worth noting that the title of the debate—"Does God Not Exist?"—was not chosen arbitrarily. It was strategically coined by the event organizer, the Tawheed Institute of New York, with deliberate rhetorical framing in mind. Traditionally, the burden of proof in such debates rests with the theist, often phrased as "Does God exist?" By reversing the formulation, the title subtly shifted the onus onto the atheist speaker to defend a negation, thereby challenging the conventional asymmetry of such discussions. This inversion invited a deeper and more rigorous exploration of both belief and disbelief, and served to stimulate critical reflection from all sides of the audience.

The Debate Transcript[1]

Opening Statements By Dan Barker

Thank you Mohamed for that very entertaining introduction, very nice. I also want to thank all the other organizers and inviters, especially Ali, who I thought was single-handedly putting this thing on, but I guess he has a lot of help with Mohsin, and others, so it's very nice to be working with such gracious people as Ali and his helpers. He is also a very generous and a very capable organizer, and I appreciate the opportunity to be a guest in this place.

There are also some freethinkers here. There are some members of the Freedom From Religion Foundation here. I recognize Irving who comes to everything in the country; members of the Atheists of NY; another member who is a student at Columbia University with some other friends there, Richard Carrier is here. So welcome to you, and thank you for coming.

There are millions of good Americans who do not believe in god. And on the planet there are about a billion people who do not believe in any kind of a god. Most of them are Buddhists, and a lot of other non-religious people who don't believe in a god. I used to believe, as you know. I believed firmly and strongly, I was a devoted disciple of Jesus. I spent many years preaching, and I changed my mind. I can't tell you the whole story. I can show you my book (Dan walks over to his table)—its not for sale today but it is available through different sources—Losing Faith in Faith: From Preacher To Atheist—going from a firm Bible believing Christian to an outspoken atheist. Or

---

[1] Note: this transcript was prepared by the organisers of the debate (Tawheed Institute of New York) and shared with Dan Barker as well.

if you rather hear it in musical form, I have a CD called "Friendly Neighborhood Atheist," with 34 songs expressing in an artistic way, my lack of belief, and my pride in being an atheist and a humanist in this world. Now I am a very happy moral person without beliefs. For me the only guide to truth is reason—not faith, not tradition, not authority and not revelation. The only way to know what is true and false is through reason.

This is an Islamic institute and I am so happy to have a chance to get acquainted with Ali and the others here; but I am not an expert on Islam, so if you want to score some points Hassanain, ask me some questions on the Qur'an because I've read much of the Qur'an, but I am not as familiar with the Qur'an as I am with the Bible. But if you do want some information that is critical of Islam specifically, and critical of the Qur'an—and criticism is good: we should all welcome criticism, because by meeting it, it strengthens our faith, doesn't it?—I would recommend to you a wonderful book I just read—by Ibn Warraq—Why I am not a Muslim. He was raised as a Muslim. He is a scholar; he was an Islamic scholar. He knows these things better than I do. So, if any of these things comes up, I have to defer to his expertise.

Hassanain, you and I have a lot in common. When you say that "there is no god but Allah," you are telling millions of good Hindus that Vishnu does not exist. Shiva, Devi do not exist; and I agree with you. You are right. Those gods do not exist. You and I are both unbelievers in those gods.

When you say "there is no god but Allah," you are telling a billion good Christians on this planet that not only is Jesus not god, he is not even the son of god; and I agree with you. The Trinitarian god of Christianity does not exist. You and I are both in agreement; we are unbelievers in that god.

When you say "there is no god but Allah," you are telling the Egyptians, the Greeks, the Romans, the Norsemen, the Mayans, the Aztecs through history there, "Osiris, Zeus, Mercury, Thor, Quetzalcoatl ... they do not exist." And I agree with you. You are right Hassanain.

Those gods that were worshipped by millions of devout believers—those gods do not exist.

The only difference between you and me is that I believe in one less god than you do.

Basically we are the same. We are unbelievers. Did you know that the early Christians were called unbelievers by the Romans, because they did not believe in the true Roman gods? Although they had their god, they were called atheists.

Atheism in its most general sense is the absence of a belief in a god or gods—atheism with a lower case "a" is not a belief system, it is not a creed, it is not a system of morality: it is simply the lack of a belief in a god, for what ever reason. Most agnostics are atheists by this broad definition, because the word "god" could mean anything, and you can't possibly disprove the existence of something that is not clearly defined.

However, when it comes to a particular definition of god, such as the Christian god, or the Islamic god, I go further than just the negative soft lower-case atheism and I make the positive claim that that particular god does not exist. In that case, I am an upper case Atheist.

Especially when it comes to the gods of the revealed religions. I am convinced and I claim to know that that those gods—the Christian god, [and] Allah, does not exist. It is not a belief; it is a claim of knowledge. The word "god" is minimally defined by the Abrahamic religions to be a personal being who created and maintains the universe, who is all-Powerful, all-Knowing, and all-Good. There is more to the definition, but in a minimal sense, that is how god is defined, and that is the god we are debating tonight.

Such a god is fictional; such a god does not exist. First I will give you my lower-case reasons, then I will give you some positive upper case "A" reasons for this claim.

First of all, it is the lack of evidence. If there is anything that is obvious, it is that the existence of god is not obvious. Even the Bible says that. "Truly you are a god who hides himself" [Isaiah 45:15], because if there is a god, where is he or she or it?

Some people say that the absence of evidence is not the evidence of absence. But I disagree. If something is truly not existent, then the only evidence we can possibly have for its non-existence would be the absence of evidence for its existence. The absence of evidence is not proof, but it is certainly evidence. If god is obvious, and if god does exist, if there is evidence for it, then why are we having this debate? We don't debate things like gravity. We don't debate things like "Who is our president," or "Does Saudi Arabia exist as a country?" We know these things by evidence. If there is a god, and if there is an evidence of a god, then why are there unbelievers, why are there atheists? Are we just blind? Are we just inherently evil? We just want to close our eyes to something that others claim is so obvious? The very existence of a billion non-believers on this planet is not proof, but it is certainly evidence. I offer myself as Exhibit A. I do not believe in a god. It is not evident to me. It is not obvious to me.

What if...what if scientists were to gather together every Sunday morning like Christians do in Church, and hold hands and bow their heads and pray and say: (Dan is singing) "Yes, gravity is real. I know that gravity is real. I will have faith. I will be strong. I know in my heart that what goes up, must come down, down, down!" (Laughter) What if they did that? You would think they were pretty insecure on the concept, wouldn't you?

That's what religious people are always doing; they are getting together—What if scientists were to get together every Friday, and bow to the north and say, "There is no law but evolution and Darwin is its prophet. There is no law but evolution and Darwin is its prophet." What if they said that over and over and over again? Wouldn't you think they were somewhat insecure? They are trying to talk themselves into this thing, for which there is no evidence. And that's what most religions do, they talk themselves into it without any actual evidence that they can show me.

Or what if [they said] "Gravity is real, and Isaac Newton is its prophet"? Isaac Newton: probably the greatest mind of science. 300 years ago he figured out the laws of gravity. Isaac Newton believed in a god and when he figured out the laws of gravity, and the orbits of the planets, and the elliptical paths and all that, it was a wonderful revelation to our world, not by revelation, but of course, by reason. He figured it out and proved it with reason.

But Isaac Newton was stymied. As great a mind as his, he bumped up against some things that he could not figure out. He did not have an answer for why all the planets were in the same plane. How could that be? Why? Or why they were all going in the same direction? And you know what the great scientific mind Isaac Newton said? He said "That is evidence of design in the Universe. That is evidence of choice. That's proof of god, the fact that they are in the same plane and they go in the same direction."

What we now know is that Isaac Newton was wrong. We now know that this gap in his understanding does have an answer. We now understand the formation of the solar system or planetary system. So we now know why they are in the same plane and in the same direction.

But in his time, it was an unknowable thing. He had this huge gap in his mind, and he said, "Well, I don't know the answer, so god is the answer." There is a big gap, and he plugged it with his god. How convenient. He had a gap in his understanding; he plugged it with his god. And that's basically how the arguments for the existence of god have all boiled down.

Christians, and Islamic and Jewish theists and others argue "Well, there is some gap in our current understanding of science, therefore, I can plug my god into that gap."

Years ago, when it was thundering and lightening, they didn't know what caused it. So, "Zeus did it" and "Thor did it." But now we understand electricity and the weather patterns, and Zeus and Thor have died. They're gone ... except we do have a day of the week dedicated to Thor. [Thursday]

Fertility of the soil. They used to wonder, "How do the crops grow?" So they had a goddess named Hera. But now we understand more, and that gap has closed, and that god has died out.

Now, I expect Hassanain is going to give some of these arguments for the existence of his god, and I will attempt to rebut them during my rebuttal time, and I have just to show that many of these arguments are basically just "god of the gaps." They are arguments from his ignorance.

I would also ask you—and I will ask you if I get a chance Hassanain—if you do expect me to disprove god, then tell me: what you would accept as a disproof?

The principle of falsifiability I think is useful. Maybe not be 100% perfect, but it is useful. For any statement to be true, there must be things that could be said about that statement which if true would make the statement false. And the failure to prove these falsifiable statements true strengthens the truth claim of the original statement.

For example, if I am a short, fat redhead, you can say "He is not a tall skinny blonde." Right? And if I were a tall skinny blonde, it would falsify that I am a short, fat redhead, right. There have to be statements you can say about your claim, which would falsify if they were true. So, I am going to ask you: give me an example of a statement, which if true, would prove your hypothesis false. What would you accept as a disproof, so then we are having a fair debate?

Now here are some positive arguments for the non-existence of god:

Suppose god is defined as a "married bachelor." Does he exist? You cannot ask "Does he exist?", but you can just say "He cannot exist." A "married bachelor" is discrepant. You can't have such a thing. And there are about a dozen different ways that god has been defined in the revealed religions that are mutually incompatible, definitions of god that cannot exist in the same being.

For example, here is a trivial example, and I will move on to a stronger one later. If god is defined as "all-merciful," or "infinitely-merciful," as I have heard some Muslims say, and if god is also defined as a "just" god, then such a being cannot exist. Because why? What does "mercy" mean? Mercy means you give punishment with less severity than is deserved by the crime. You committed this crime; you deserve this punishment, but "Be merciful to me god." So god gives you less punishment. Maybe he sets you free, maybe he is "infinitely merciful." By the way if god is infinitely merciful, then I am not going to Hell, right? (Laughter) If he is infinitely merciful, no one is going to go to Hell. That's a side point.

But to be just ... what does it mean to be just? What is justice? "Just" means that you have the punishment that fits the crime. You commit the crime, you get this punishment. That's justice. We want justice in world. But if god is "all-merciful," "infinitely merciful," then he can never be "just." If god is ever "just," only once even, then he cannot be "ALL-merciful." He has to be "sometimes merciful," and "sometimes just," but he cannot be "all merciful."

So, it follows, a god who is defined as "all-merciful" and "just" not only doesn't exist, but cannot exist.

Here's a stronger one. God is defined as a "personal being." To be a personal being you have to be able to make decisions. Which means you have to have a potential of uncertainty. Tomorrow I am going to decide something, but before then I could change my mind, right? So I am a free, personal being because I have the ability, at least in principle, to change my mind. If I didn't have that ability, then I would not be a free agent, a personal being. But god is also defined as "all-knowing." He is defined as "omniscient," which means that not only does he know about the past, present and the future of everything, but he also knows all his own future decisions. If god knows all of his own future decisions, and if the set of future facts is fixed by his omniscience, then that puts some limits on his power, doesn't it? He is not able to change his mind between now and then. He has to go like a robot or a computer program. He is stuck. If he knows the future he can't change it. If he goes ahead and proves his power by changing it anyway, then he was not omniscient in the first place, was he? So this is a short-hand version of saying that a god who is defined as "personal" and "all-knowing" not only does not exist: such a god cannot exist. He either has freedom, or he doesn't. And if he knows the future, he has no freedom. I call this the Free Will Argument for the Non-Existence of God, or FANG for short.

Another problem—another "married bachelor" problem—is the idea of an immaterial mind. All we know about minds is that they exist within some kind of a physical housing: a human brain, a computer or something. We have no evidence or no coherent definition of a mind or spirit that can exist apart from something physical.

Another evidence for the non-existence of god is that all these god believers claim virtually without exception that believing in god makes you a better person, makes you more moral. Believing in god is how you can live the good and right life. But when you look at the lives of believers, you do not see better lives. you do not see—Muslims are not more moral people than atheists. They do not love their children any more. They do not provide for charity anymore. Muslims, Christians and Jews were just about the same. In fact in America, non-believers score better than Christians do on lot of these moral charitable things. And If there is a god who gives us absolute moral standards, why do no believers agree on what they are?

Take the death penalty, for example, or abortion rights, or gay rights, or euthanasia, or women rights, or doctor-assisted suicide, or stem cell research—you name it, you will find devout, praying god believers falling on both sides of those issues. God believers do not agree with each other, so where is this absolute morality? That doesn't disprove god, but it is an evidence against the existence of a god who gives moral standards.

Another argument against the existence of god, of course, is the problem of evil. All you have to do is walk into any children's hospital, and you know there is no god. Children are in pain, they are suffering, their parents are desperately praying for god to protect them. They are praying, "Jesus"—or "God, or Elohim or whoever—"protect my child." And the children die. They don't survive. Occasionally, according to statistics, some of them will get better, prayed-for or not. And of course the believers think that's proof of prayer. But in my family we had a traumatic situation, where my wife did survive, not because of invoking prayer, but because of invoking good medical attention.

On September 11 [2001], Hassanain, those god believers who committed that act of terrorism had a foreknowledge of the evil that they wanted to do. They had a belief in a god, they had a belief in a Heaven. And It's not only Muslims, but its believers of all stripes who commit horrible acts. What if you had known what was in the minds of those terrorists? What if you would have known about it in advance and what if you had the ability to stop it, without any risk to yourself? Would you have stopped them? I would have. I am sure—you are a good man—that you would have stopped it. You would have stopped the bloodshed, the trauma. I would have, as a good human, moral person. If you say "Yes, I would have stopped it," then you are nicer than god. Because god had the foreknowledge, god had the power to stop the brutality, but he did nothing about it. In my book, he is something of immoral accomplice.

Also, besides these evidences for god's non-existence, I don't see any need to believe in a god. You can live a good moral life, a happy life, a reasonable life, a compassionate life. Even Jesus said, "They who are whole don't need a doctor." Well, most of us atheists consider that we are not sick. We are not sinners. We do not have this need for some master up there before whom we can bow as a slave. And we can live a good life without a belief in a god.

So, my time is up, Mohamed tells me, and we will now move to the next phase.

Rebuttal By Hassanain Rajabali

I begin in the name of Allah, the Beneficent, the Merciful.

Without taking too much time, I will make a formal introduction when I begin my presentation. But due to limited time to rebut I will just spend a few moments in just sort of listing these issues with regard to what my friend Dan has spoken about.

It's very similar as I see that your arguments that you have brought forth with regards to the non-existence of God as you have used in all your debates—with (Dr. Phil) Fernandes for example, and others you have debated with, and it seems that you—you have got all your arguments laid down on your website too and it almost seems like a dogmatic presentation in trying to refute the existence of God.

So let's go with the basics here. First you say, that you use reason. Absolutely, reason is a very necessary tool by which mankind needs to ascertain the realities, for if one were to remove reason from his tools then he fails to reach his goal. You say that there are a billion people who are atheists—well I think you have taken it a little too far—because a Buddhist is not an atheist, he's what we call a non-theist. He does not reject the existence of God, he simply defines it differently, in a different manner. We can discuss that later.

When you say that you claim knowledge and not belief, I fail to understand how a person can come forward and say that there is no God and say that I don't have a belief. It's a claim of knowledge you say but it's not a belief. And I don't understand that difference. When you say lack of evidence it's amazing that in all the debates that have taken place between the atheists such as people like—Bertrand Russell, as you all revere very much, the atheists that do, you find that this argument of design is so conspicuous, its staring and glaring at one's nose, that yet you simply say—well this has to be discarded as just a mere existence of some primordial soup that came into existence out of nothing with nothing, by nothing, through total probabilistic game. This is absolutely impossible; impossible from all standards of logic and reason, as we would say. So the interesting fact is that, yes, reason is a necessary entity, but something that is so prevalent, that is so clear about the system of design in the universe and to reject it, and simply say that it has no purpose, no design, no meaning, it just came out of nothing, going nowhere with no meaning, I think that is really, really stretching the issue, way beyond reason—it becomes totally unreasonable, and that's the question.

So, you asked me; you mentioned for example, Isaac Newton—you said he was a great scientific mind, but he was wrong because he couldn't answer some of the things. No one denies that a human being, no matter how brilliant a mind is can have an understanding of everything. It's not possible. There will always be some level of ignorance in the reality by which we live in. The universe is vast—it is not possible for us to understand everything. That does not preclude the fact therefore that I have to reject in a Maker.

When Isaac Newton said what he said, that may be he was wrong, but he said that there is a design; it did not imply that because—in other words he knew 80%, 20% was not known and on that 20% because he did not know he used that 20% as proof that God exists. That's not true. What he said is that there is a designer, but there is this much that I do not understand. Whether we fill the gap, or we don't fill the gap has no relevance to the fact that the reality exist, but you have not answered the rest of the question. Just because we don't know something does not imply it is not there. So for someone to say that if Isaac Newton says something which he makes a wrong scientific judgment—everybody makes a wrong judgment sometime in life, but that does not imply; that they therefore abandon the whole system, and I think that's where we are coming from.

So when you say something is falsifiable, how do you prove for example, what do I expect from you? The very basic question we are debating this issue is—if you and I did not exist—why would we be debating? The question here has got nothing to do with anything further than our existence. We exist; we want to know where did we come from. What is our goal? You mentioned in all your debates, in your arguments, with regards that you know we are moral people, we are good people, we do good things, (and) we give charity. I fail to understand why. Honestly, and I like if you can give me some explanation on that. Why would you do that? You came from nothing, you have no goals, you are going nowhere, you have no goals, why for this transient period of time, are you so concerned about coming forward and telling the world that God doesn't exist—I fail to understand this. Really, I am being very concise on this matter, but when you say it's a falsifiable, falsify my existence. I challenge that. Tell me that I don't exist—because the minute you discuss your existence and my existence, you and I have to go back and question the integrity of where did we come from, and that brings me to the next question.

I've noticed for example, you speak about God. We call Allah God. What is Allah? From Islamic perspective, Allah means the God, the Absolute, indivisible God. The Holy Qur'an says *Qul huwa llāhu 'aḥad*—Say God is unique, one, *Allāhu ṣamad*, God is independent, he depends on nothing, everything depends on Him, *lam yalid*—He does not beget, nor is He begotten, nor is He born. So for someone to say that God had a son, or sons, or sonship, as you mentioned and we agreed on that—that we don't accept that. This absolute God has no frame of reference. Frame of reference implies something that is bound within time, matter and space. The problem with these arguments is that we keep constantly debating on the issue of bringing God to the relative world. The relative world cannot exist without an absolute Creator, and that's the argument.

You keep arguing on the issue of God in the relative sense. God is not transient; He is the "Necessary Existence". We are the transient existence. Meaning that you and I can exist or not exist. There is an equal chance as one would say, that a person who exists—who is dependent, couldn't cause his own existence. It can tip either way. There has to be a higher necessary existence that is the immovable mover, who is not bound in time, matter and space. So every time you ask about matter, is God a mind, is he thinking? Does he have gray matter? That again is a matter of relative discussion.

When we say that God is bound in time, how did He know tomorrow—tomorrow is not a substantive matter to question about God. God has no tomorrow. He knows, His knowledge is infinite in the absolute sense of the word, and absolute cannot be defined, but we understand it indirectly, for this relative universe can never exist without an Absolute Creator.

You speak about infinitely Merciful God—God IS infinitely merciful, but the problem once again is you take one dimension (attribute) of God, meaning the justice of God, and then you envision it in a pinhole mechanism, in a relative sense. You 'compartmentalize' His attributes, and that's where the problem comes. And that's typical—not only for you, but even for believers. Among the Muslims there are people who say God is infinitely Merciful, that means that everything that I can do is okay, because in the end He is going to forgive me anyway.

From the Islamic perspective, there are 99 attributes given to God. The attributes are not separate entities of God. You and I as human beings are limited in our perceptions and concepts. We are compartmental creatures. We cannot think simultaneously—multiple times, in different dimensions at the same time. Thus the limitation is ours, and this infinite God is communicating to us due to our limitation. And our limitation should not imply therefore that we take our limitation and apply it on God. And that's a clear indication that when I say God is Merciful—when Qur'an says God is Merciful, and God is Just, these simultaneous characteristics cannot be compartmentalized, we must understand them holistically and the holistic nature that we can understand and which the Qur'an tells us through revelation is sufficient to indicate that a universe that is so magnificent, that has endowed every creature with its power to exist.

And even an atheist, as you know, yourself also, that when you become ill, you go to the hospital to get yourself fixed because life is so precious to you. It's amazing that you came from nowhere, you're going nowhere, yet life is so precious, you make every effort to make sure you live. And that alone is sufficient indication for man to say—what's wrong with you?? Haven't you seen this wonderful system created in you? So you're talking about (the) infinite Mercy of God—yes, the 'mercy' is infinite.

The fact that you and I have the power to even discuss is the Mercy of God. The fact that you and I have the power to reject is the Mercy of God. The fact that you and I have the power to obey is the Mercy of God. That's what we see as infinite Mercy. When you say justice and mercy cannot exist together (and) that's once again—if you put it into a dimension of a relative world, it makes sense, but God is not relative, He is Absolute. So thus this question is not possible.

Final point is when you say about Evil—and I will answer this question—you have asked this question to all your previous people (debate opponents) with regards to children dying, how, would you have stopped him, would you have stopped him??? Yes, I am under a trial, if I could have stopped September 11, I would have but "God is not under a trial." So it is irrelevant for him.

Reply By Dan Barker

Buddhists are atheists. They don't overtly, positively reject a god, but they are atheists by the general definition of what it means to be without belief.

I know this was a rebuttal, and I am waiting to hear your positive arguments. Therefore, I might withhold some of my remarks, until I hear your positive arguments.

But your whole concept of design illustrates my point about using a gap. The fact that we don't understand at this time all of the nature of the design in the universe—does not give you the freedom to just plug that gap with your god.

There are many people who feel that the universe is poorly designed. There are many people who think that there is a lot of cruelty and ugliness built into the universe. Built in the human genome, there are some horribly designed sloppy things built into our system. So to claim that the world is gloriously designed is a burden of proof that you must share, because many of us don't see it that way. We see ourselves in spite of the lack of design.

And Isaac Newton explicitly said that these two things that he did not understand were evidence of design. He said that. He didn't say that there is a gap in his understanding. He basically said that this is evidence of choice. He was using the gap as evidence. Which is what theists like to do, which is what you like to do, find the gap in our understanding.

The question is, what's going to happen some day when the gap closes? What's going to happen when we go—"Oh we do now have a complete cosmological picture"? When that happens, will you reject your belief in god? I doubt it.

I think you are using these arguments more as an excuse to pretend to be an intellectual. But if these gaps close, of course, you will find some other reason.

And of course, it is a relative discussion. We all know that the world that we live in is relative. I am not claiming any type of absolutes or even a transcendence. It is all relative. If you think that there is some absolute frame of reference in a theistic sense, then it is up to you to show that, not just assume that maybe it could happen.

During your opening statement, I assumed you would give us evidence for—not just evidence for our ignorance—but evidence for your claim that there is this all-powerful personal being up there.

One of your last comments underscored my opening statement quite nicely. Another one of the "incohesive" arguments against god is that, to be a person means you have limits. I am not a redhead. I am not a big, tall, fat guy from Buffalo, New York. I am who I am. We define ourselves as who we are, where we were born. We have limits, and our limits are what define us. But a being who has no limits, who is not compartmentalized—as you claim your Allah is—cannot be said, then, to be a person. Because there's no way to know what is not him.

A person has to be a limited being in someway. So if god is infinite, if he is totally unlimited, then he is not a personal being. Then he is an "infinite blob of nothingness." Basically, you are defining him out of existence. To define god, you have to define what he is, not just what he is not. Thank you.

Opening Statements by Hassanain Rajabali

I begin in the name of Allah, the Beneficent, the Merciful, the One who created everything with utmost perfection. There is no imperfection in his creation, and that which we see as imperfection is our own ignorance, and not the system in itself. Thus for someone to say that the universe is imperfect, one has to admit that it is their mind that does not conceive it properly, and the system that the mind did not conceive it properly is the part of a perfect design. So for one to reject that would be tantamount to putting cart in front of the horse. So, the perspective here with regards to the debate that we are having today, is Does God not exist?

We put this burden of proof obviously on Mr. Dan Barker because it is essential that in order for us to disprove the existence of God, one has to somehow from the materialistic perspective come with an empirical observation and disprove the existence of God. One can say that "Well, since I can't measure God, therefore there is no proof in the existence of God." But that is not the reality. The fact is that we exist and there is a higher dimension by which our existence comes from is a sufficient proof.

Steven Hawkins in his book A Brief History of Time, explains that this singularity of the point that this so called Big Bang took place, as we know, we cannot go further than the Planks Constant of one times ten to the minus 43($10E-43$), because all physical laws that we understand cease to exist.

Who brought about this grand Universe? The universe which

functions so intrinsically, so interwoven, that even scientists who studied black holes out in the universe understand that they have an effect in my existence in this world.

This concept of the Anthropic Universe, the Holy Qur'an upholds it very clearly, it says *'Alam taraw 'anna Allāha sakhkhara lakum*— do you not see that God has made for you subservient this whole universe—*mā fī as-samāwāti wa mā fī al-'arḍi*—whatever is in the Heavens and in the earth, it has been made subservient to you. One might say then "is the whole universe just for me?" That is not the implication. The implication is that the universe has been created for my benefit also.

Whether I am the central figure is not the issue of the discussion today, but the question to say, is the existence of God or the non existence of God. When you say about the non-existence of God, how would you prove the non-existence of God?

The fact that you and I exist, is the question you and I need to ask. How did we come, and this is the typical debate that takes it right to the very basics and says where did we come from. There's disagreement in all different schools of thought, among the atheists themselves and the agnostics also as to where does all start? Is it a steady state universe, whether the universe has always been here, well that's all been disproved by the very founder—Fred Hoyle. So, you find that is not true.

Is the universe expanding and contracting? Do we have an oscillating universe. That does not seem to show proof at all from reason and from empirical evidence that this universe is contracting and expanding with its mass that it cannot sustain itself. So the obvious question is that we know that the universe is expanding. We can see that. It has been observed.

When you talk about the Doppler Shift and you look at the Red Shift, you can see that the universe is expanding—there is a constant expansion. This expansion has a direct implication on my existence on this earth.

When we talk about the issue of design, my friend Dan mentions that I have not brought enough evidence. It is not my platform here to bring you an abundance of arguments. There are plenty of them, voluminous, but the interesting irony is that we do not even need that. In this grand universe, I have this capacity to produce sound, to breathe, to think simultaneously, to move and have depth of perception. If you are going to reject that as design, then you are begging the question because essentially it does not convince me rather than saying–well, I am not willing to be convinced because I want to shut my eyes, and I want to be lied.

When you can say that how can you prove the existence of god—first of all, we exist in this universe. The design and the probabilistic factors make it impossible scientifically and empirically for the universe to come into existence the way it did.

With reference to Planck's Constant of one times ten to the minus forty three ($10E-43$) when all the basic fundamental laws were set in motion. We talk about natural selection—this argument is constantly brought (discussed). Natural selection is an entity that is part of the great design. You seem to have taken this thing (theory), and the pin hole vision of how an engine in the car does combustion and said "that's it, we don't need to worry about the car itself, it is the combustion within the system that takes place, and that's sufficient for us." Well, then that in itself is an incredible design.

To reject design, is once again begging the question. In all the arguments that I have heard, that takes place with an atheist, these issues of design that have been brought forward in numerous ways, is so sufficient, that due to lack of time we don't need to bring it forth, but if you need it, we can spend 10, 15, 20, or 30 minutes as much as you need on this subject, and we discuss all these aspects of design, and for you to refute even one of them and take it out of perspective, and say it is not needed in this grand holistic universe, then we are begging the question once again.

Just going very quickly in describing our position as Muslims—so that at least we are on a better platform and there's no confusion. When we talk about Islam, what does Islam say with regards to God? God is Absolute. You asked this question just now and said "Absolute frame of reference." A frame of reference implies that there is a position by which something is, for example, in Science I can't say this room is 500. 500 what? 500 yards? 500 miles? 500 kilograms? What is it? What do you mean? I need a frame of reference.

A Human mind cannot function outside (of the) frame of reference. It's impossible. And that's where our limitation lies. The fact that we are so bound within the frame of reference, we are having a problem in these discussions. But God is not bound in the frame of reference. He is the creator of time. Time is a creation of God. Matter is a creation of God. These are transient entities. Transient entities cannot come into existence by themselves. Nothing can exist from nothing with nothing by nothing. That is not possible. That means, that our existence, had to have pre-existed a necessary existent—in Arabic it is called *wājib al-wujūd* ; the necessary existent that brings forth all transient (*mumkin al-wujūd*) into existence. And that the *mumkin* (transient) cannot demand its own existence, nor can it demand its own non-existence. It cannot.

That's very important to understand. When you talk of a frame of reference, we must clearly understand that, when we ask questions about God in time, knowing the future, we have to be very careful in how we define this terminology, for God's knowledge of the future, of my future, is Absolute in His domain. He knows everything but He is not bound in the time where He is experimenting himself for He is not bound in space, time and matter. Those are created entities which He has put into it. So for me to put him into it, would also be very wrong.

When you say "Infinite Blob of Nothingness," that's a contradiction in statement and I think it is just a matter of rhetoric.

Let me spend a few moments with regards to the issue of "Evil", as you mentioned, and what is our position from the Islamic perspective.

God created this universe out of his infinite mercy. The Holy Qur'an says—*kataba 'alā nafsihi ar-raḥmah*—he has made incumbent upon Himself (it is metaphorical), that mercy is upon his creation. We're all (his) creation. That's why, when I began my presentation, I said, "I begin in the name of God, the Beneficent, the Merciful." Now, one might say what kind of a God is this who brings pain and difficulty. Let me explain this very briefly without taking too much time.

First and foremost, we have been created to be tried—the Qur'an clearly states that "Mankind has been created for a trial". This trial is not for God to know, it is for man to know. In other words, when I am under trial, though God knows exactly what is going to happen to me, and it is not for Him to know what I will do.

When it comes to "free will", a human being has "free will", he has been given total authority to choose his own destiny, but God knows this "Destiny." And knowledge of God about his free will does not imply the fact that because God knows he has caused him to do it, those are 2 separate entities here, because, in the absolute realm, once again, he is not bound in time and we have to take that into perspective.

We are under a trial, human kind has been endowed with intellect. The Qur'an mentions it beautifully—*laqad khalaqnā al-insāna fī aḥsani taqwīm*, we have created man in a perfect form. What does that mean? The Qur'an says *wa nafsin wa mā sawwāhā*—This self, (or soul) in me has been perfected, *fa-alhamahā fujūrahā wa taqwāhā* and it has been taught wrong and right. So when the common atheist says, "I have this morals in me, I know what is right and wrong". Exactly!! The creator has planted that into your soul. And it is the beginning platform, that when the human being says that you never communicated with me on the day of Judgment, you say "No, that is not correct." It was implanted in you and you know what the moral goodness was.

And when we discuss morality, you will see this whole concept of "free thinking", atheism and agnosticism in its truest form. It is wiser for an atheist to say that he is an agnostic, instead of saying that he is an atheist.

You say that we are not certain about this universe. We don't know. Then I fail to understand how can you take a stand and say there is no God. You yourself admit, that there is no design, we don't understand all the dimensions of it. So how come you have taken that step, leap forward, and said, "There is no God." Therefore, you should subject yourself to the same scrutiny, and you should say "I have not enough evidence, and I cannot make a legal claim."

A man comes to the Holy Prophet (s.a.w.) and says, "I am an atheist". Prophet asks "Why?" The man said, "I believe the universe has always existed, and will always exist, therefore there is no God. Prophet asked, "Why is it? " The man said, "because I have never seen a God create it". Prophet asked, "Have you seen that the universe always existed and will always exist?" The man said "No." The Prophet then said, "How come you have taken one side over the other. It is wiser for you to say 'I don't know,' and I will subject myself to further scrutiny, than to take a stand and say there's 'No God' because you have taken that stand and you have no evidence."

In fact if you look, it is very bold for someone to say that there is 'No God,' considering yourself to be so bound with this intrinsic system, which is so magnificent. That, I think is an interesting thing, from the Qur'anic perspective. When you read the Holy Qur'an you will find that there are very few verses with regards to the arguments against the atheists. In fact the Holy Qur'an only asks the question, "How can you reject when you were created, you will die, and you will be raised again. Do you not see?" as my brother Abbas Peera recited Surah al-Rahman, "we created you, which bounties of your Lord will you deny."[1] All these wonderful things we created for you. It is so inherent that there is no need to get into semantical arguments, polemical arguments and then say, I need to debate this. Look at you! You have

---

1 This statement in the Surah appears at least 34 times! (Ed.)

negated something that's so obvious.

And as you mentioned in your presentation before when the Christians say, "Oh gravity come down what goes up comes down". Yes it is absurdity! Precisely! That is the point from theistic believer, that when you reject this fantastic design, that's absurdity from that perspective.

So in retrospect, when we talk about the whole concept of Islamic perspective, we are under trial. We have been endowed with intellect and free will. We have been given the choice to accept or reject our own destiny. This is what the trial is all about. Now, let me explain. When a teacher gives an exam, your implication is, why is there evil in this world? What is evil? From the Islamic perspective, there's no such thing as absolute evil. Absolute evil does not exist—it is relative—and it changes its position depending on which side you take, and which angle of perspective you take.

That which is good for one side can be bad for another simultaneously as is the case in a relative frame of reference.

I can say that I can be extremely larger with relations to an atom, and at the same time, I am extremely small with the relations to the universe. It depends on my frame of reference, when things change positions. Thus when we talk about relativity, when we talk about good and evil, they take positions inside but nothing in the universe is absolutely evil. There is no such thing.

An absolutely perfect God does not create an imperfect system, nor or is there such a thing like evil, in its absolute sense. Let me give another example, lies versus truth. You will find that to lie is evil and to speak the truth is good. You will see that lies cannot exist without the truth, but on the other hand, truth can exist without lie. For example, if I say, I always lie. Does it make sense? No. Because there is no essence of truth in my statement, thus it becomes nonsensical. Therefore, truth is a necessary constituent to lies. But I can certainly say that, "I always speak the truth", or "I sometimes speak the truth", it makes perfect sense, because there is an element of truth in my statement, and thus my statement makes sense.

Thus when it comes to the relative perspective within the Islamic position, that is what it means. When Allah says, *min sharri mā khalaq*—by the evil or by that rejection. What does 'Evil' mean from the Islamic perspective? It means that which lacks good. It's just like 'darkness'. It cannot exist. You cannot measure darkness. It is lack of light that you can measure. You cannot measure coldness. It is lack of heat, because it is only heat that our senses measure, not coldness.

So from the Islamic perspective, it is a relativistic position, and evil is a trial. When evil comes into play would we say that when a teacher gives exam, and each question has 5 multiple choices, and only one is right, and four are wrong. From that perspective you say that one of them is a good answer. If you select the right one you get rewarded, and if you select any of the other four, it is evil, because you get punished by getting a zero for that question. Now, would you say that the teacher is inherent to evil for having put four wrong answers to one right answer? Or would you say that the exam is so preposterous that evil absolutely outweighs the good. Would you say that the teacher should remove all evil, and make all answers correct? In fact, you will say that you are fooling me—you are now shaking my own foundation—that you are actually insulting me. Either give me the exam and allow me to select my own ways, and to see the difference between the good and the bad, the right and the wrong, or else, don't try me.

Trials, if you look at them, are an inherent part of our existence. No human being on earth—theist or non-theist—exists outside the realm of an exam.

Today we are being examined by this debate. Why are we doing this? Because we want to find out what is right and what is wrong. If the wrong did not exist, would we be able to debate? No! And when you see that we want to discuss this issue, absolutely discussing and bringing it forth with the power of reason and having an open mind is very essential. But to condemn unequivocally, just because one things rejects to you, then you are pushing it a little too far.

I like the academic discussion here, when you say there is plenty of evidence and let us look into it further, rather than saying, that is it! The Qur'an mentions they reject it because they want it that way, they wish it that way. But the reality dawns upon them. But the Qur'an is saying, from Islamic perspective we are under trial. Evil is a relative entity and it is a trial by which mankind should appreciate the good.

When you see a child dying, yes, it is sad. But what if a child could not die? Let's take that perspective. If you chop the head of a child, and it does not die, he's still alive, it's immune from all disease. That would be the state of preposterous mentality. What system is this that I can abuse and kick the child like rubber ball because no matter what you do with it and nothing happens to it. But if something happened, God is evil, and he allowed the baby to die. Is it a catch 22 or a circular argument? No. The argument is for you to appreciate a healthy baby, one needs to have a relative perspective by which to understand good. Good cannot be understood without that which is not good and is existing simultaneously.

We're relative creatures, and that is how we understand things, and we can never have a conception of something that is bad, until we understand what is good. That reality, that co-existence is a necessity in this world. If one wants to say that evil should not exist, then earth should not exist. You and I should not exist, trial should not exist, and exam should not exist. Rather we are in a system where we understand that evil is there.

A lot of the evil that takes place on the earth is man made. It is not natural. However, if you look at natural disasters such as an earthquake—an earthquake, for the greater good is good for the earth. When it releases its heat from the center of the earth and the fact that it shakes, it is good for the greater good.. Thus, should we say that we should eliminate all earthquakes and let man survive. No !! From the Islamic perspective, this trial world is transient, it is for a short time period, and within this trial when you die, that is just the beginning of this existence.

What follows after? Allah says many a times in the Qur'an, "we created you from nothing, what is to prevent us from making you again. We can bring you into existence just like that, and take you into non-existence just like that." It means nothing to God. It is nothing. He (Allah) says, "You walk with pride, thinking that you are so intelligent with your scientific observation." Look at the scientist. He is so proud, he is a great thinker. What has a great thinker done? Nothing, except observed. He has not created anything, he has not invented, he has only observed.

When you say Isaac Newton observed gravitational forces, he simply observed and he became a great man. Imagine the one who put the gravity there? No, that's out of design, we say. We revere people—(loud applaud from the audience). When we talk about this, however we cut it, we have to examine this from the perspective of Islam. Evil is something that is under a trial.

The Qur'an mentions that be patient and understand that your reality, your dogma, your system, has a higher good and your trials and tribulations in this world is part of this exam. In conclusion, you would never say that the teacher is evil when he/she examines a child. Nor does a teacher give an exam for the teacher to know what the student will do. No. The student goes to the university and takes an exam for himself to know, how much he is capable so that he can use that in order to get a better salary out in the real world. It is not for the teacher to know. Therefore, for one to say that God needs to know—right here, is the very simplest example one can give, that in an exam without that which is evil, and it is not a part of the system, it cannot be an exam. It is tantamount to removing it from the entire system. Thank you.

Rebuttal by Dan Barker

Thank you Hassanain. You have a good gift of teaching and you are a good man. He is a good man. I think most religious people are good people, in spite of their Holy Book, and I applaud all the good that Christians, Jews and Muslims do in the world.

But I think your opening statement basically proved my point, and you also are attacking a straw man. I have never said that I reject design. You must have been reading another debate.

There is ample evidence of design in the universe, and we can account for that design in natural ways. There is design by Natural Selection. When you look at the ridges of the sand dunes, when you look at the design of how molecules combine because of the limited number of ways geometrically they can come together, that's a certain design by the laws of nature. Yes there is design, and your argument about design basically amounted to what I said in my opening statement: a "god of the gaps."

Here's your words, "Where did we come from?" [that] you gave as an evidence for god. That's a question. Right? That is not evidence. Surprisingly, you find this book [Qur'an], this ink on the page, which tells you where we came from, and you plug that question with your particular brand of a god. Theists have been doing this for centuries, for millenniums. They have been plugging that question with their god. So, you have not given us evidence for a god; you have given evidence for our ignorance.

I claim that there is a lot of design in universe that can be explained in natural ways. It is a beautiful, wonderful design, and it is right here in our own backyard. It is not some transcendental mystical thing out there. But think about what you are saying.

If functional complexity and design requires a designer, or multiple designers made it—the human minds is complex, and look how we exist: we function, we feel we are moral, how our eyes function—if all this design is within us that requires a higher designer than us, because we could not have designed it ourselves, right? Well, think about this: is not the mind of Allah beautifully organized? Doesn't it function with purpose? Does it not have a goal? Does it not have some kind of inner-working of desires, wants, needs goals and purposes? Is it not also beautifully designed? Or is it some random jumble of transcendent ideas?

In order for you to worship your god, you have to assume that your god is a purposeful being, that your god has a mind that functions in a logical way, somehow. Your god makes a decision, [in fact] that decision that does not happen in the reverse. There's some logic to it. The mind of your god is, as you say, beautiful, wonderful, organized.

By your own reasoning, then, if functional complexity requires a designer, then the functional complexity of your designer also requires a designer.

God needs a designer himself. Otherwise, your logic is wrong in the first place. If your god's design does not require a designer, then neither do we.

It is you who is begging the question. Because, suppose there is a god up there, sitting up there in the Seventh Heaven or wherever it is, and saying, "I am here, and I have desires, and I think I will create some worlds and people. But, I exist. And according to you (Hassanain), we should not even question our own existence—right?—without having some frame of reference outside of ourselves." What gives your god the freedom then, to say that "I exist, but I am not going to question my frame of reference. I just exist."? The logical question is "Why, and how?"

How did this god come into existence? If he does exist, if he is functionally complex, if he is beautiful, and if he acknowledges his existence, then you are simply answering one mystery with another mystery.

You are not answering the question; you are simply delaying the question. "We do not understand our existence, therefore there is a designer up there." The designer if he/she asks the same question, comes to the same problem, and we atheists prefer to stop with what we do not know. We do not prefer to unnecessarily multiply hypotheses to say there must be something greater, because it does not answer anything. It doesn't give us any evidence for.

You say, in the Qur'an, "we atheists reject it because we want it that way." That is untrue. The Qur'an is wrong. I do not reject the belief in god because I want it that way. If there is a god, I will accept, I will believe. If there is a god, it would be foolish of me not to accept. I don't want it that way. It's not a matter of what you want—in fact you seem to be betraying that there is a religious bias between people.

I could say that "You believe in god, because you want it." But that doesn't answer anything. That amounts to ad hominem in the argument. You are attacking me as a person, rather than the evidence, by telling me that it is my inner weaknesses and my inner desires of not wanting god. That is unacceptable in a debate to attack your opponent's motives. If there is a god, it doesn't matter if I want it or not. I want the evidence for that god to exist.

You say "Nothing comes from nothing." So, is god something? Well if god says "Nothing comes from nothing," and if he is something, so how could he even exist?

Think about this: how many ways are there for something to exist? Lots of ways, right? How many ways are there for nothing to exist? Only one. So, which is more likely, that something exists or nothing?

Why do we assume that reality, if left unperturbed, would somehow default to the state of nothingness? As if that were a thing. Obviously, something exists, and even if god exists, god is something, and "something existing" is a brute fact of reality.

The whole concept of nothingness is an incoherent concept in itself. Even as you were pointing out, somewhere we need to refer to some brute fact and we atheists say, "Well, existence exists. It's here, as far as we perceive it to exist."

"God is on trial. God claims to be omni good (omniscient). He claims to be all good." If a teacher in a classroom is giving an exam to students and the teacher sees one of the students hurting in one way, and refuses to help, then that teacher is guilty of some kind of an accessory to the continuation of that student's pain. You (Hassanain) admitted that you would stop (the tragic event of) September 11. So would I, and so would everyone in this room have stopped it. So, if your god is all good, he is on trial. You see the point of the problem of evil? He claims to be all good, and you claim that if you pray to him, he will answer your prayers, but repeatedly, your prayers are not answered.

He apparently cares more about the free will of Christian, Jewish and Islamic terrorists, than he does about the precious human lives, which could have been saved. You say it is a test. Evil is relative? So in god's mind, September 11 could have been good? According to your reference, if evil is relative, and it's a "lack of good," then in god's mind, September 11 could have been a good thing. You are telling us that there could be a mysterious higher way that something like that could be justified—and I say that kind of thinking is morally bankrupt.

To excuse anybody—your master, your slave master, your Lord, your teacher, your god—because he/she is "good," and has a higher purpose, that is moral bankruptcy, and it removes you from the field of criticism. It removes you from the ability to say "I disapprove. I denounce."

I will say that if your god or the god of the Bible does exist, and if I am forced to meet him some day, then I will denounce him to his face. I will say, "You are a brutal god. I do not respect your actions. You caused harm and you could have avoided harm, and you didn't."

As a moral human being, I have the obligation to say that to a slave master who bosses me around, the slave master who tells me to bow down. So I think that we naturalists have a firmer grasp of what it means to be moral than believers who just simply close their minds and say "whatever the father wants is what we get."

You used the word "judgment" in your statement, and the word "judgment" basically boils down to Heaven and Hell. Again I will say—Heaven and Hell—Hell is a threat. Hell is an intimidation: "Do you want to burn?" The Bible and Qur'an are filled with these examples. I am going to get a double dose of Hell because I am an unbeliever, right? That's a threat to me, a physical intimidation on my person. That's what that book is.

If I don't follow the way you people think. I will repeat: any system of thought, any ideology that has to make its point by threatening violence, as the Bible does, and as the Qur'an does, is a morally bankrupt system.

We can find a natural way to be good to each other by minimizing harm in the natural world. By being kind to each other. By being good to each other in the natural world, in ways that we know to lessen harm. We don't need a Daddy in the sky to tell us what to do. We all know it. We didn't need the Ten Commandments to tell us there was something wrong with killing. We could have figured it out on our own, as we did long before the Ten Commandments.

Reply by Hassanain Rajabali

In this few minutes I would like to make some quick points. First and foremost, when we say we want it from the Qur'an, that the atheists want it, the want and the need is an inherent fact of all creatures. That is not what I said. I said the want for a believer to want to have an understanding of his own existence is equivalent to the one who is non-theist / atheist who wants to understand his existence too. The want is not in question. It's how we come to the conclusion. I am not saying that we have a desire for a want. We are manufacturing the conclusion.

In your rebuttal you completely ignored the entire issue of design. You said yes there is design. Yes there is wonderful design but I can say that it's a natural selection. Or that is the natural movement. It is interesting that you are accepting this incredible system, but you do not want to go further than natural selection. Natural selection is part of the greater. And you have limited yourself within a scope of a greater, and you say this is all I am going to focus on. I am going to ignore the greater.

Natural selection cannot exist by itself, it cannot demand its own existence, it's part of the greater system, and you don't want to answer that question, and I know why. The minute you do, you are going to have to question the integrity where did you come from. I have absolutely every right to say like every human being to find out where did we come from.

For you to say the idea of gaps, the god of the gaps, for you also to say that there is no god is also a gap. I think your gap is much wider because for one to say, because of this incredible design, therefore there is no maker, no designer. But then you turn quickly and say, if everything has a design, and the design has a designer, then the designer has a designer. Well I told you earlier, and you apparently did not understand.

In the relative world there is that transit nature of the design system. But the absolute creator is the immovable mover, who is not bound in that design. You have not come to the absolute domain, and challenge me on that perspective, that this absolute God does not bound in matter, time and space cannot be questioned in this integrity, and you keep questioning that integrity. You are saying, God you've written this article, dear Theologian. Honestly Dan, with all due respect, you say we are good people—we atheists are good people, we are kind people, for what you write, have you ever taken into consideration that there are those who believe in that theological ideology? That you are bashing them so face forwardly, almost in an instigating fashion. You could say, how about me, how come I am not so academic? You say, you know what, this is what they, that's perfectly fine, rather than make satirical fun of God, that I am so lonely up here, I know nothing and if I read that theologian for you, you've written it, and if the public were to read it, and if you read it, it really is very insulting to me, and I think as an academician, like yourself, I really admire the fact that you have come forward and posed this question, and I like your pattern, by which you say I want to understand—that's wonderful, and I respect you for that and for that reason I am debating with you.

The reason is that when arguments come down and when the substance of matter comes, Quran says—*Qul hātū burhānakum in kuntum ṣādiqīn*—Tell them to bring the proof, if they are real, if they are truthful, bring the proof and put it on the table.

Nothing comes from nothing, I did not say that. I said nothing comes from nothing with nothing by nothing. That is what I said. So you have misquoted me there. You said teacher verses God. You say God is on trial, once again you put him in a relative world, and you put him on trial. God is the Absolute Creator, He is not under trial, He has no deficiencies. So, for you to say he needs to go on a trial, implies that there is a deficiency, and that's not acceptable. You said—I will not accept God because He is forcing me to bow. You are naturalistic, it is interesting, you are bound by gravitational forces, you are bound by a gender to be a male, you are bound by your two eyes, why aren't you angry with that?

Why don't you say, I am a male, and I am being forced by natural laws to be a male, to breathe oxygen, I cannot breathe nitrogen, I cannot breathe under water, I cannot reverse my time, I cannot reverse my age, I cannot stop my birth, why aren't you angry with those things? And you are a naturalist, and I love these things, and I fail to understand that.

Questions from the Audience

Question #1: (For Dan Barker)

"You have stated that you are a moral person. What is the foundation for your morality? Where do you derive your morals from? And what evidence can you provide that your moral system is good and correct?"

Dan Barker: By definition morality means the lessening of harm. If people increase harm, by definition they are immoral. If they unnecessarily increase harm in the world, they are immoral people. We can use the word "Evil" as a kind of tag for that. Morality by definition is then the minimizing of harm, and that's what we all mean.

If we do things that makes harm less, then you are a moral person. And as a corollary, we can say enhancing life, compassion, and adding to understanding. If morality is basically the minimizing of harm, none of us want to harm. Do we? We all want to raise our families where we all want to be free of pain. Of course, then the question becomes not "Where do we get our absolute principles?" The question becomes, "How do we identify harm?"

What is harm? Harm is a natural thing. Harm in its identification, in its avoidance are natural exercises. If this were a cup full of arsenic, and I handed it to Hassanain, then it would be a harmful act. But if it is a glass of water, and if I handed it to him, well, then that would be a good act. If he is thirsty, I assume he is thirsty. So harm is relative to our human natures and the environment we live in, and its avoidance is a natural exercise. And most of us have good enough minds—unless you are unhealthy in some ways—to know how to do this. And a lot of this is common sense.

A lot of moral dilemmas involve a conflict of values. It's not always "Should I do this?", or "Should I not do this?", or "Should I do this or should I do this?" I have two or more courses of action, in which case it becomes an exercise of assessing their relative merits of the various consequences of those acts in trying to decide which one of those leads to the less amount of harm. And even if you fail, if you intend to lessen harm in the world, you could be called a moral person.

The problem with absolute morality is that you will do what is "right" or "wrong" because of some absolute mandate, not because you evaluated the consequences.

Response by Hassanain Rajabali: First of all, I have a difficulty understanding with your definition of morality. It seems to be very self-centered, morality where the individual is—I am good, therefore the world is good. I like good things, therefore the world likes good things. This ideology of morality which is self-centered, can never be a social ideology, that can never be legislated under the sphere of social beings. You for example, yourself say, in your website say there is no universal moral urge, and not all ethical systems agree polygamy for example, human sacrifice, cannibalism, wife beating, all these are perfectly moral actions in certain cultures. Is god confused? Your implication therefore is that polygamy is wrong.

It has got nothing to do with harm. If three women get married to one man—to you that is harm. I don't understand how you came up with that conclusion, but when you say for example, to call God contradictory, there is no higher moral good that comes from this ideology, and it can never be legislated.

Question #2: (For Hassanain Rajabali)

"Why is it necessary to believe in god? Want god treat all equally good men, equally, regardless of race, sex or creed?"

Hassanain Rajabali: God creates everything with perfection, everybody is endowed with his or her abilities. You will find that insects are able to protect their own environment and live. Animals have their own environments by which to live. If you observe the Discovery Channel today, where all those interesting videos are being displayed today, shows the grand scheme of things where this Creator has endowed every creature with the ability to sustain its life and therefore it is able to procreate, and sustain in this incredible universe. So the existence of God is a necessity, because everything in this universe is a transient existence. It cannot demand its own existence.

Therefore, it requires what we call a necessary existent, and that is the one that has brought existence. So, do we need God—yes. Not only for our existence, but our moral codes are derived from that too. There is a higher, longer focus for human beings, ethical standards, the deed that I do today is accountable in the hereafter. As far as unbelievers, an atheist says, committing a perfect crime is a good deed, as long as you don't get caught, it's fine.

Response by Dan Barker: I think that missed the point of the question. If I am a good and moral person by your standards, then if you judge me to be a good moral person, but I don't believe in a god, is it right for your god to punish me for the simple fact of unbelief? That was the question being asked.

Why is it necessary to believe, if we can live good lives? And you have to admit that many atheists and agnostics live very good lives, and many theists live horrible lives. Right? Many people who believe in god live horrible lives.

So the question really is, "Why should I be punished in eternal Hell for simply living a good moral life as you live?" That's unfair. Any god who has that type of a system is not a good god, is not worthy of my worship.

Question #3: (For Hassanain Rajabali)

"Why do Muslims need to follow a book of religion if there is a God? Wouldn't there be some real signs and absolute directions to man and God's helper accepting responsibility for his actions?"

Hassanain Rajabali: God creates a system where he gives man free will and that free will allows him to decipher wrong from right. The differences that we (humans) have in opinion is a prime reason to show that we have free will. If everybody was thinking the same and there would be no ambiguity in any issue that the implication would be that it is a defeated purpose for the exam itself is not an exam in its truest form.

And you know, in any exam, the greater the difficulty of the exam, the greater the value of the exam. The student who passes, deserves a greater reward. So when you say, that there is a moral god, this god that we follow, he gives us the laws, divine laws are essential—what we call 'Our Guiding Light', and an individual who says, like Dan says I am a good person, there's nothing wrong with me, why would God punish me. If a student goes into class, and refuses to observe the rules of the exam, and says, I am a good student, will the teacher say but since you are rejecting the exam, the teacher say I will pass you. I don't understand that.

Response by Dan Barker: My only response is that I am being condemned for eternity in Hell for the simple fact that I do not believe, not for something I have done. Atheists, agnostics and humanists say that people should be judged by their actions, not by their beliefs.

Beliefs don't make you a good person. There are many devout believers who commit horrible actions. So, it is wrong again to say that just because I don't believe is somehow breaking a rule. What sense does that have in a rule—"Believe!"—when you can still take the exam without believing that there is a great exam maker in the sky? You can still get the questions right. Can't you? You can still live a good life, without the belief.

If I live a good life without the belief in your God, and your God wants to punish me forever for the simple act of not believing in his existence, that's unfair.

Question #4: (For Dan Barker)

"Science cannot and will not explain everything. Thus there will always be a god of gaps. Don't you agree?"

Dan Barker: Yes, except Science is closing a lot of doors. There were questions that were [once] open. For example, Darwin did not understand genetics. He did not understand DNA. And if Darwin had ... he would have closed the gap in his mind. Yes, we have closed some of those gaps, and science is progressing.

And who is Isaac Newton to say that we would never understand the formation of planetary system? And who is Hassanain to say that "We have now reached the end of knowledge. All of these gaps will never be closed again."?

I will ask you the same question that I asked you before: What happens if the [windows] gap would be closed? What happens if we have a cosmological explanation of the origin of the universes? Then will you reject your belief in god? What happens when we do have a perfectly natural understanding of design apart from the question of whether it is absolute or relative trials, then when that gap is closed, will you reject your belief in your god?

Is it really an honest argument that you are making or are you coming to the argument with your belief in God first, looking for gaps to plug? Sure, science does not know ... there are a million things that we don't know. That's what drives science. If we didn't have that uncertainty then science would not be driven.

Atheists and agnostics welcome the uncertainty. We like not knowing. We don't have to invent some answer. We like having debates and argument and disagreement because that's what drives the pursuit of truth.

Response by Hasanain Rajabali: What you're saying with regards to Science, first of all, you've taken the assumption that Science answers everything. How does Science answer the power of reason, the power of love, the power of hate, ethical questions, and morality. Where in Science within the five senses in the empirical observation can you tell me that Science has ever delved into the question of moral ethics?

You can never get the answer. Science is limited. The reason I am saying you can never get the answer is because you have limited yourselves, within a certain set of tools which are in itself limited, and that you're saying that only this tool is going to give me the answer, when itself is limited, then I can say without any hesitation that you will never get the answer. First and foremost, Science is limited in its scope, that's why you see Scientists don't talk about the existence of God. Because within the empirical observation you're not allowed to even say that.

Also Steve Hawkings says that this is something that the philosophers' talk about, we scientists are simply empirical observers. What you make out of it is your issue.

Question #5: (For Hassanain Rajabali)

"If humans need a reference to go forward, then shouldn't God come within that reference for us to understand him."

Hasanain Rajabali: God is the Absolute Creator, He has no frame of reference. Thus to put him in a frame of reference implies that He is limited, and in reality God is not limited, that's why he is not in the scope of reference. For you and I, as our Prophet (Mohammed, peace be upon him) says—*Man 'arafa nafsahu faqad 'arafa Rabbah*—If you know yourself, then you will know your Lord—and that power of the self-introspection and knowing who you are, in an indirect fashion is sufficient evidence. Even Dan himself says that "In a direct fashion of reasonable thinking where you use logical explanations in an indirect fashion, you can ascertain things." For example, if someone says "I Love you", well, can you define it? Can you display it to me? Is it quantified? Can you ever observe it? Never! It comes in an indirect fashion.

When someone sacrifices himself (or herself) under difficult conditions then you say "Aha!" that person loves me. No one has rejected the existence of love, but it is not a directly observable entity the same as the power of reason, and there are many entities as such that are not directly observable, and sufficient evidence is to say that the relative entity cannot exist by itself, without the absolute.

The Absolute has no frame of reference, thus to defy the system and to say that God therefore should be relative is begging the question. When you say, why does not God come in a human form? For argument sake, yes, if He came, what would be the requirement of this "Human-God" that you would approve of, (If he had) two eyes you (would probably) say I wish he had three eyes, if he had three eyes (then you would say) I wish he had four eyes (and if) he has no eyes then you would say (I wish) he had no eyes then I would worship him. What you essentially want to do is to bring him down to the relative earth, so that you can deny him. And that's the problem, that God is not a relative entity, and the fact that He is Absolute, overwhelms the human mind and that is sufficient for one to submit.

Response by Dan Barker: I disagree. Love can be observed. It can be studied. It can be measured. Love is a verb; it is an action. If I am abusing my wife, there's an indication that I do not love her. If I am burning my children with fire, there's an indication that I do not love them. The fact that I provide for their needs, that I meet them, spend some time with them ... love is something that we do observe and measure. Many scientists are addressing the moral questions. You are wrong to say that scientists are not addressing moral questions.

Right now, I am reading Matt Ridley's book The Origin of Virtue. I just read Steven Pinker's book The Blank Slate, addressing the human-nature instinct to compassion and to reciprocal altruism, and the evolutionary genetic advantages to those things within our species. Science does address these things and comes up with good answers for what you think are mysterious questions.

Question #6: (For Dan Barker)

"If an atheist can live by a moral code, then how do you explain the killing of millions of human beings by the greatest atheists of all times, Lenin, Stalin, Mao Tse Tsung, etc."

Dan Barker: Well, most atheists don't say that they live by a moral code. A code is something that is codified. It is a list, just like you have a list of 10 commandments of "Do this" and "Don't do that."s Few atheists would say that they live by a moral code. Most of us say we live by moral principles.

As I elaborated earlier, the principle of minimizing harm in a natural world is a principle that works for us. That's what morality means. Yes, atheists have done horrible things, no one denies that.

Atheism is not a creed or a religion. Just as many Christians are shocked at how some of their co-believers have murdered abortion doctors, and they say that does not represent all Christians. Think about Stalin, for example, who was seminary trained, or think about Hitler, who was a Christian and a member of the Catholic church—think of some of these people. Were they doing it in the name of atheism, to promote atheism, or were they doing it for political reasons. Were they brutal tyrants for political personal gains?

Of course atheism does not pretend to make you a better person. Atheism never says that. Atheism is simply the absence of a religion. But some of us atheists feel that the absence of a religion is still superior to the presence of an absolutistic moral code in which if a god says "Kill", you should kill, and it is right, because god says it's right. And that is immoral. So, I am not going to excuse Stalin or Pol Pott. I am going to denounce those actions as immoral because they cause unnecessary harm.

Response by Hassanain Rajabali: Well, first of all the question is that you cannot legislate what you just said, you said that "We do not have a moral code", so, how did you condemn it? You condemned it on an individual level. Not on a social level.

You can never legislate this condemnation because what Stalin and Marks did has no correlation to your basic moral codes, because you have no basic moral codes. So how can you say "Legislate it?" How can you vociferously say, Dan Barker may say "Yes", another atheist may say "No", what Stalin did was very good.

This is a anarchistic mentality that appears as a result of a person who says, there is no moral code. You make it as you go, you are a free thinker, no one tells you what to do, do what you want, when you want, how you want, no one is your boss, you are your own boss. Essentially then, the sadomasochist is one who would like to inflict pain, and the masochist is one who likes to receive pains. If they became our global leaders, it would be perfectly justified as to what Hitler did. As a result when you say, there is no moral code, this in itself is a danger.

Question #7: (For Hassanain Rajabali)

"I as a relatively ignorant Buddha (Bojhwa)?? believe that I cannot know if God is a reality. Furthermore by the ethos of my background to take a stand one way or another way would be an act of arrogance—Are you willing to consider the possibility that you cannot know even if you consider it for a short time."

Hassanain Rajabali: A person who is not endowed with enough understanding, comes into that position that he cannot know. And that's a perfectly reasonable argument. And at that state, you have every right to say that I don't know, and to limit yourself in the state of suspension, when you say I am not certain, but that does not preclude the fact that you should not therefore search for it, because the evidence is sufficient, plenty of evidence. It's equivalent to saying that, we don't know about this theory, or we don't know about this existence that does not say that therefore in the world of science you should not go out and delve into the depths of universe and find it.

That finding of the self is so inherently important in this entire discussion, we are not talking about matter out in space, we are not talking about planetary bodies out in space, we are talking about ourselves, our ethical issues. Even Dan agrees with me, that we are moral creatures, we condemn. We believe, when you say I don't believe, we atheists are non-believers. No! you are believers, you are a believers in a system, and a system accepts certain things, and rejects certain things.

To monopolize a word and say, I am not a believer, it is the system of—Eric Frohm who was a German philosopher—the question is not whether you have a religion or not, the question is which religion do you have. Rejecting God is a religion, it is a way of life, it has its effects on all human beings. That person who is an atheist, becomes a President, becomes a legislator, he is going to instill his ideology upon the people. You cannot be a creature in limbo, floating in space with no ideology, and to take that position and say—look I am not harmful, I am not doing anything. But here, Pope Paul, as we mentioned, Carl Marx—millions of people were killed because of that, can we say therefore they were wrong? By whose standards? By their standards they're atheists, who can tell them wrong. They have no moral codes, I got away with it, and it is perfectly fine.

Response by Mr. Dan Barker: To say that atheists are unbelievers in God is not to say that atheists have no beliefs in other things. Atheists can be fiercely committed and have a belief in the equal treatment of women, for example and denounce the mistreatment of women in most of the revealed religions. We can have a belief—that it is better for humanity if men and women are treated equal. It doesn't follow that if we do not believe in god, we don't have any beliefs. I never said that. So there's another strong .....

You also did add another ad hominem, Hasanain. You said to those of us who are "not endowed with understanding," which basically is an attack on me. Somehow, you have more understanding. What do you know that I don't? Is there some secret thing about the world that you know, that I don't? You are "endowed with understanding," but I am not? You are the chosen one, but I am not? You are special, blessed, and I am not? You have vision, and I am blind? Is that what you are saying? And only those who are blessed with superior vision and intelligence ... it's really a very self-centered thing to say. Ad hominem attack is not acceptable within a debate.

Question #8: (For Dan Barker)

"If god does not exist, then how do you recount for that inner voice that each of us possess scientifically. How can you explain this? Isn't this beyond our relative realm?"

Dan Barker: Well, an "inner voice" can mean a million different things. Sometimes when I am stressed for staying up late for 2 or 3 nights, I might hear my mother's voice in my mind. Carl Sagan said he used to hear the inner voice of his parents talking to him. It is a natural thing that happens, when the brain sometimes goes into certain states. I know a man who "talks to Jesus" all the time, and "Jesus' voice" is very clear to him. And he says that he is a baritone. He knows that Jesus is a baritone because he hears his voice.

People who hear voices I don't think are good arbiters of truth. I do not have an inner voice for morality. I simply have a principle that says "Stalin was wrong, not because he broke some code, not because he didn't follow a list of do's and don't's. Stalin was wrong because he caused harm." That's simple to understand, isn't it?

Hitler caused harm. We all know what harm is. He didn't have to [cause harm], and he did. So I can say, based on the relativistic definition of what morality means—we are human beings who want to survive. We recoil from pain, by nature. You stick your hand in fire and you pull from it. You don't need some code to tell you "Thou shall pull thy hands from the flames." It's our nature to recoil from pain.

So, if we're going to use the word "morality," we are talking about the natural harm in the natural world, and I can denounce Stalin on that relativistic principle that he could have and did not minimize harm in this world, and therefore he was what we could call, with a lowercase "e," an "evil" person.

Response by Hassanain Rajabali: When you say cause harm, if a man goes to battle, and he is fighting, and he gives his life for the cause of the greater, he caused harm to himself by his own death, yet we call them heroes. So it is very relativistic when we say "cause harm", when you say "cause harm, killing for the greater good", how then would you define the greater good? What is the greater good?

If a battle takes place between two people then there is harm. Therefore, what do you do then? Do you just simply prevent harm? How will you prevent harm without causing harm to the other side? So when you say we do not cause harm, it is a very loose and vague term. It is not applicable, it's not practical. I am not rejecting that we should stop harm. But the question here is that you can not apply it in a legislative fashion. You cannot apply it on any social arena because we are very individualistic, and I think that's where the problem lies.

Question #9: (For Hassanain Rajabali)

"If an atheist offered a reasonable explanation for why the universe exists and for all evidence of design, would you conceive that there might not be god after all?"

Hassanain: You are asking a question which is really an impossibility by its own nature. If you say that there is a reasonable answer (explanation) for no creator, the reasonable answer (explanation) first of all, you have to jump over the basic hurdle of asking yourself, how does a relative universe come into existence by itself. Whatever that answer that you're going to give me has to be God, whether you want to call it God, that whatever the case may be, Supreme Power is what we are discussing. How you name is based on your own perception. But the question is that the infinite power is a necessity, anything less than that has been created for centuries, anything less than that is not sufficient.

Response by Mr. Dan Barker: So you are saying that theoretically you would allow for the possibility of an impersonal transcendent supernatural force that's not personal. You're saying that you would allow for the possibility that the universe came into existence by some supernatural means that is not necessarily a being that we can worship. You would allow for that theoretical possibility then?

Hassanain: No

Dan: You just seemed to say that

Hassanain: No, I did not.

Dan: If you are saying it is impossible for a non-personal being to have caused the universe, then I say you're begging the question. I am open. If you can give me evidence for a god, I will change my mind. If you can give me evidence for Allah, I will change my mind and we will believe in Allah—I will do that. But you have a close-minded position.

You have boxed yourself into a corner saying, it is an "Impossibility." Those are your words. Therefore, you're not open to truth. You're being dogmatic in your position. Convince me, and I'll change my mind. I've done it before and I will do it again. And I would like to hear you say the same thing: that you would change your mind, if the evidence warrants it.

Hassanain Rajabali: I wish we had the cross-examination ...

Question #10: (For Dan Barker)

"You say that scientists don't know everything, can you also say atheists go by the code of inflicting the least harm. If you yourself do not know everything, you are not in the correct position to decide what inflicts the least harm. What do you say to that?"

Dan Barker: Well, I said it before that by definition, morality is the intention to minimize harm. That is what it means. We are not even discussing morality unless we have a definition. So by definition, what do we mean by morality is that you cannot be just following orders. You can not take the Nuerenberg defense and say that I was just doing what my boss told me. We have to use our minds. I said before that most moral dilemmas come when you have a conflict of values, not when you are just trying to decide "yes or no" on this, but when there is a conflict of values. If your intention is to assess the merits, the relative merits of the consequences of these different actions, and thereby to compute what would be the least amount of harm for those two actions, if that is your intention, and even if you fail—because we don't know everything—then you can be called a moral person.

I might commit an act that I think to be moral, and due to my ignorance, I cause more harm ... I will feel horrible if I made a mistake. I would hope to learn from it. That's what moral education is: we learn from our mistakes. But if my intention was to minimize harm, whatever that means, whatever the level of my education and experience and knowledge is of the facts, then I can be called a moral person.

If my intention is to increase unnecessary harm, then I would be called an immoral person. I would be called even "evil." I don't like these absolute words, "Good" and "Evil," but we can use them as language tags for the intention of a person to create harm in the world where it is not necessary to be created. I agree with you that there are no clear answers either way, but we can legislate morality if enough of us get together, enough human beings get together, and say we don't like what Hitler did, then we can make laws to try to stop Hitler.

There's no big mystery to that, and if enough of us get together, on some of these issues that aren't such a gray area, then we can make a legislation. And legislation is fluid. In our country laws change and they improve over time. But in religious morality, laws have no room for improvement.

Hassanain: You say I am closed minded—Yes, if you say that I am rational, I am using logic, I am using evidence and observations, then yes, you might say that I am close minded.

To answer your question—you mention the law, if you say something and say it's wrong, well, then the law will recognize it, was my mistake. You've not defined that law. It is arbitrary, you see it comes into existence in your mind and then it disappears. It is almost like you are creating it to justify something, then it disappears again.

If you say if enough people come together and you can justify, so if Germany did what it did, the majority of Germans believed in the removal of the non-ethnic race. Then from your moral standards, what Hitler did, and his people, and what Saddam is doing today in Iraq is sufficient evidence to say that they're morally right. That just begs the question.

Question #11: (For Hassanain Rajabali)

"Could you please elaborate on the Islamic perspective of evil and Hell as a natural consequence of one's own action and not of god's making."

Hassanain Rajabali: Hell is something you and I earn due to our own rejections. And Dan, before you take umbridge, when I said you have a lack of understanding I never implied it to you. Don't take anything personal. It's nothing to take personal here. It is not implying that you are ignorant in any way, we are having a discussion in this matter, and I did not say, the question was that if I have a lack of understanding, can I suspend?

I never said it is you who has a lack of understanding. In fact you have not suspended, you have taken a position.

To answer your question with regards to the position of evil from the Quranic and Islamic perspective, mankind has been endowed with enough evidence and enough gifts. For him to reject that system is tantamount to be punished. Just like a teacher who punishes you after having taught you, and you fail the exam. That punishment is a natural consequence, no one says this student failed, you are being unfair, you should pass him. Well then, you are degrading the entire system.

For someone to go to Hell, understand that their dimensions, it is not our platform to discuss this, but I would love to have that discussion. But the issue of Hell is something that human beings earn. The Qur'anic perspective is those who go to Hell will say—it is because of our own misdeeds. Had we listened, had we obeyed, had we accepted what was given to us that was so prevalent, we would not be the inmates of this punishment, and that punishment is needed on the basis of the great mercy of god, given to man to live in perpetuity in the paradise, and for someone to say that this is…… called the golden pot, look how every human being functions in that system.

We're goal oriented. We go to work, because we want to get paid at the end of the week. Should we deny that? You're saying deny that, have no acceptance of any pot at the end of the day. That's preposterous. We are living in this system, if God has created this system, and we're within it, it does not mean he created Heaven and Hell, in order to provide ourselves the moral codes. Even as a father you say to your child "Don't do this, this will happen." Why do you restrict your child from doing it? Because you know there is an impending danger in it. God is giving us this standard to follow. There's nothing wrong with it, it's perfectly fine.

Response by Mr. Dan Barker: Does it ever occur to you, Hasanain, that if there is a Heaven, and a Hell, and if Heaven is getting to live for eternity with the god of the Bible, or the god of the Qur'an, and if some of us have examined the actions and the intentions of that god and we find it to be beneath our dignity, as moral people—does it ever occur to you that some of us might prefer Hell to living in Heaven with your brutal dictator who creates such harm?

Some of us might think that was a moral thing to do. I won't mind spending eternity in Hell if it was a better moral act. Let him prove what a Macho Man he is and send me to Hell and torture me forever simply for the crime of questioning his motives.

So I take my denunciation in Hell as a form of a compliment, and I thank you for the compliment. All the good people in Hell, like Bertrand Russell, Elizabeth Cady Stanton, we're (all) going to have some great conversation, while you are up there, bowing down before your Master Lord. Think about our choice. I have more dignity.

Question #12: (For Dan Barker)

"Many a times we make meticulous plans but yet they fail in the last stage. Who overrules your plan?"

Dan Barker: Many times we make meticulous plans and it falls apart. It happens a lot of times. This debate is one example. We had a few minor glitches. Most of us unbelievers are somewhat pragmatic about the world. We know that things aren't going to happen exactly the way we plan, and we are not gods. We don't pretend to have perfection, we don't pretend to be omniscient, we don't pretend to be all-powerful. We accept our human limitations in the natural environment in which we live, and sometimes things will not go according to our plan, because we are not all-powerful.

And I don't care, as long as I am intending to do the best I can. If I fail somehow, if plans go wrong then I will learn from that mistake. I hope I will learn from that, if I am open minded. That's what happened with Christianity. I preached for 19 years, and I studied it more closely, and I learned, "Oops, I made a mistake. This is the wrong religion. This is not for me."

Ibn Warraq did the same thing with Islam. He lived the Islamic (Muslim) life, and yet he studied it closely with the eye of scholarship, and gives excellent reasons for why he changed his mind. Things did not go exactly as he planned. He thought he was going to be a faithful Muslim his whole life, and he started studying the evidences, started looking at the criticisms, (and then) he realized there is something better than this.

Response by Hassanain Rajabali: It's interesting you say that a person like Ibn Warraq takes that position. Because a person lacks understanding and takes a position, that does not imply anything in anyway. When you take for example the position that you've taken, with regards to the moral codes once again, you have not justified a social system. When you say you are promoting this anarchistic ideology, that every human being is a free thinker on his own, and as long as 51 people out of a 100 sufficiently decide on something, as we call it democracy, it becomes moral. That's taking democracy to a higher level, where we say it's moral now, and that really is deadly in its very system. When a person says, "Well I have a free thought, and things don't go right the way they do," that does not mean you abandon.

From what I read, Dan (Barker) from your perceptions, the statement you just made "this terrible god" you seem to have a lot of anger. And if that is anger, then I think you should vent it out differently.

Question #13: (For Hassanain Rajabali)

"If there were god why would it put people on the earth to waste their time frame?"

Hasanain Rajabali: Waste their Time! There is an assumption that what we are doing is useless and that in itself is a negating question. A person who prays, is praying for his own good. Science has even shown, even those who don't believe in God, that those intercessory prayers and those people who pray on their own, according to research done, that people who are in the hospital bed, themselves praying for, not others praying for them, have a higher rate of cure than those who don't. That means prayer is shown to be a very good entity.

When someone prays, it is for himself (or herself)—it takes them to a greater moral grounds. When a person submits himself (or herself), gives himself (or herself) into charity, to goodness, controls his animalistic behavior, becomes chaste and a good person—I don't see how you call it (prayers) a waste of time.

Prayer is good for the individual, God does not need prayer. Prayer is a means by which to reap the wonderful mercies of God and to negate that is tantamount to disconnecting the jugular vein of the individual.

In today's modern world, children are not taught about God in schools, and observe what they are doing. Humans are made of material and spiritual. If you deny them the spiritual aspect they will go and fill it up... Today there is a problem in the United States with devil worshipping—all types of ridiculous behavior—in trying to reach the realm of the unseen. It's human nature. To deny it is to choke it. Therefore, prayer is very good—for one to say it is a baseless act—that is total ignorance in a statement.

Response by Mr. Dan Barker: You need to look at this. Dr. Richard Sloan and others have done a careful study on this so-called "intercessory prayer" study, and showed that they are all flawed. Everybody agrees that relaxing during recuperation can help someone's recovery. No one agrees that praying will restore a lost eyeball, or a lost arm, or will get rid of cancer. No, that never happens. But if you are recovering, and you need lower blood pressure in order to recover, then prayer in connection with your faith, and your community, whether you're religious or non-religious ... like what happened with my wife when she almost died in the hospital. She found support from her community of non-believing community, family and friends. And that helped her to recover better.

But prayer as a way to cajole some ... God to change laws of nature to my benefit, that never has been shown to work. Nothing fails ... [like prayer] ... We all know that prayer is a failure, except that it can make you feel better and recover a little faster in some types of medical recuperations.

Hassanain Rajabali: So, you do agree.

Moderator: This brings to an end of the Question and Answer session.

Closing Statements by Dan Barker

Thank you for sitting through this long event. Great will be your reward on earth for that.

As I said in my opening statement, Hassanain, you and I have a lot in common. You and I have virtually identical DNA. My blood can be used as a transfusion to save your life, and vice versa. My children could breed with your children. Somewhere back in time, you and I have a common ancestor. Each of us has been physically cut from our mothers. We know that. We are basically one huge physical organism. You and I are truly brothers in the same species.

My dad is a Delaware Indian (Lenni Lenape Indian). My ancestors' homeland is right across the Hudson river—where there's now New Jersey—before we were forced to leave our homeland because of the Christian-European invaders who came with a weapon in one hand and a bible in the other claiming that it was God's will to chase us off—similar to what the Christian-European crusaders did to the Arabs, which I think was morally wrong. They had no moral right to go over there, to try replace one religion with another—and somewhere [else], in my own personal opinion—not all atheists agree—but similar to the way the Christian-European Jewish settlers came into that area and tried to make some religious claim to the land.

I think we should stop building these walls. I think we should stop drawing these circles. You have a circle that you are in. You are a respected man, and a knowledgeable man, and in a certain circle in the world, but outside of the circle are the infidels, the believers—it is "we" versus "they," "us versus them," and those "out there" are our enemies.

My mom was also a part Apache Indian, although she had a grandmother whose last name was "Sopher," which is some kind of a Semitic name, or Jewish name. Maybe we have a common ancestor who is closer than we think. Who knows? Her parents came from Spain. May be it was 10 generations ago you and I had the same ancestor father and mother. That makes us one.

The Bible and the Qur'an are apparently your source of information about this god you worship. It didn't just come out of the air. Both books, if you read them—and I have really enjoyed reading some of the Qur'an, though I am not an expert in them —but if you get to the bottom, they both are really books of war. They are books "versus them," fighting. The god of those books is the God of War.

And I think to have any hope for our world, we don't all have to convert to atheists. It is not my mission to try to convert you to an atheist. I think there's little chance of that happening, right? I don't care in what you believe. I don't care if you believe in Allah or stand on your head and speak in tongues in front of Mother Goose. I don't care. This is a free world.

In America, we have a separation of religion in government where the government backs off and says you are free to believe what you like even if everyone thinks it is stupid. Even if you think atheists are stupid and evil, they are free to be atheists in this country. We need a system in this world where we stop equating religion with government.

I don't see what is to be gained in my life by believing in a god. I don't see what I get out of that. Maybe god is so hungry to be praised. I mean, would you worship me if I stood up and said you should pray to me everyday? No, you wouldn't do that. You'd think I'm some kind of a mean..... sick guy who was born and wants to be worshipped and praised all the time, with little servants down there who bow down and say "Yes, you're great."

If there is a deity up there, what do I gain from believing in it? As I told you, Hell doesn't scare me. The threats of punishment do not scare me. I want to live my own life. I want to live with good natural principles.

I heard that religion is a way to offer you to live a good life. Here is what we atheists say:

"If you want to live a good life and be kind to others, then live a good life and be kind to others." If I am motivated to be kind to others by the threat of Hell, then that shows how little I think of myself. Doesn't it? I need some help to be a good person. I am no good.

Or if I am persuaded to be kind to others by the promise of Heaven, well, then that shows how little I actually think of others. I am doing it for selfish reasons. I want to go to Heaven, I want to be cuddled by this daddy up there who is going to make me feel good and give me things.

Both atheists and humanists in this world say: "Let's be good, for goodness' sake."

Closing Statements by Hassanain Rajabali

Thank you Dan (Barker) for your closing arguments. I will just make some very quick points here. First and foremost, what we get in conclusion to this debate is that we see that those who hold this free thinking mentality, this free thinking concept of life are lawless people—let me explain what lawless means as I don't want to be taken out of perspective. It means those who are not socially bound in any law system, as Dan has mentioned, "stop building these walls, let's break them down." What you are saying is that take all the laws out, take all institutions down, dismantle them, because they do nothing but harm. Well, if you dismantle them, will you live in a lawless society? Is that what you're promoting? Or are you saying dismantle them and rebuild? When you rebuild then, you just built them again. Which one has the higher goal?

When you talk about the universality of our existence, you say that we are the same, yes, we are the same and that's the ingenuity of our existence that if a person is asked to program something where it can take every parameter into possibility into action, that a person's mind and thought decides to do something with this application, you ask the programmer what a heroic task that is.

It's an impossibility to put all actions together where a person has his completely open architected system, where you take atoms and combine them, you shift one molecule over another, change the bonds from one place to another, and it changes its clarity, and it causes harm or it causes good. That universality in itself is sufficient for you and I to submit ourselves, that "wow", it's not so enclosed, it is so universal, that we share so much together, that it all works in consonants that an incredible Creator had to put this together for all of it to work together, that in itself is sufficient evidence for anyone.

We don't have to get into polemics, into rhetoric's, into discussions, it is sufficient for yourself to see in the mirror, and say "Wow!", to reject that is tantamount to saying I don't want to see it, and that's fine, it's your choice.

What I am getting completely from this debate—when it comes to morality—is make it 'yourself'. You yourself said on your website, "everybody is a free thinker, no one tells you anything, not a Rabbi, not a priest, not a politician", but you didn't add one thing—Not an atheist either. You didn't put that in there, because you're saying to yourself that we should have our own thought, and I'm telling you how it should be. Well, then you should. You negated your own purpose. Because, when you say you shouldn't impose any law to anybody, then you shouldn't even speak about it. You should be silent, and let every man think for himself. But that's not the case.

You said that the Bible is our source! Correction—(Only) The Qur'an is our source. The original Bible which was revealed to Jesus was a perfect book. It was adulterated, we do not accept it. We accept it as a revelation to Jesus, Jesus was a great Prophet, he was a great man, and he performed many miracles. Qur'an upholds it, and we have no doubt in it, no questions.

In conclusion we say the Qur'an is our litmus test. It is the criterion. It is what decides right from wrong. Science is subject to it. The higher authority, the one who created the Universe, has put Science into motion, and to take one aspect of the greater and to say that is my God is a very foolish statement.

You say I don't care about people praying. Yet I see so much anger in your statement. You say "I don't care if a person wants to do this, or if he wants to do that," yet, you have made so many condescending statements that you're praying to this vicious God, or you're fooling around. You make even funny statements about people bowing their heads on the ground. When I read that, it is a clear indication to me that you're angry. You're angry with something, rather than having respect for somebody who wants to worship his own God, why don't you say "let him worship". Yet on your website you say "We should forbid worship of God in school. It's a public place. It is our tax dollars". Well, then you are promoting rejection of prayer in public. See! There you go. You see the actions co comes to the practical indications.

When it comes to individuals, in conclusion, the individual 'knows his Lord' A man comes to our 6th Imam (Imam Jaafar al-Sadiq, a.s.) and says, "tell me about this existence of God." He (the 6th Imam) asks him, "What do you do for your living?" He (the man) says "I am a sailor". He (the 6th Imam) said, "When you travel have you had those moments when you were floating on that piece of wood, and your life was in danger?" And the man said "yes". He (the 6th Imam) said, "Did you have that glimmer of hope? he said "Yes". He (the 6th Imam) said "That's your Lord! That's inbuilt into you."

I'll give you an example, my uncle was flying on Air Tanzania, and the plane was primarily of Chinese people, who were atheists, and the pilot said that the landing gear was not opening and that they were going to do a belly landing. He saw all these Chinese were murmuring something. Then the gears opened up, and it (the aircraft) landed safely. My uncle asked them "What were you murmuring? You are atheists." They said "Yes, we are atheists. We were murmuring about that hope". My uncle said "But you don't believe in it." They said, "But then we did."

In conclusion—when you look at the atheistic perspective, you find that there's no time factor, a final point—(you said) let's be good for the sake of goodness, (I say) let's worship God for the sake of God. Thank you.

Brief Commentary

Opening Arguments

Dan Barker, representing the atheist position, began his opening argument by offering a definition of atheism that emphasized the absence of belief rather than a positive denial of God's existence. He stated, "Atheism is not a claim to knowledge, but rather a position of non-belief due to insufficient evidence." By framing atheism as a methodological stance rooted in skepticism and empirical validation, Barker distanced himself from ideological atheism and instead positioned his worldview within the epistemic traditions of science and reason.

Central to Barker's critique of theism was the assertion that belief in God often rests upon "gaps" in human understanding. This is commonly referred to as the "God of the gaps" fallacy, wherein divine explanations are invoked in lieu of scientific or rational clarity. For Barker, this strategy not only stifles intellectual progress but also introduces unnecessary complexity into our understanding of reality. "If you're going to postulate a God to explain the universe," he argued, "you must then explain the complexity of that God. And this simply kicks the explanatory can further down the road."

A key feature of Barker's argument was the Free Will Argument for the Non-Existence of God (FANG). According to this line of reasoning, if God is omniscient and knows the future infallibly, then human free will is effectively nullified. If God already knows one's future choices, then those choices cannot be otherwise, and hence moral accountability becomes incoherent. Barker contended that the very theological premises that attempt to justify God's nature unravel under logical scrutiny. This argument served a dual purpose: it not only questioned divine omniscience but also challenged the consistency of religious moral frameworks based on free will.

Barker also highlighted the Problem of Evil, raising questions about the coexistence of an all-powerful, all-good God and the presence of gratuitous suffering in the world. Using real-world examples such as terrorism and natural disasters, he posed the dilemma: "If God is willing to prevent evil but not able, then He is impotent. If He is able but not willing, then He is malevolent. If He is both able and willing, then whence cometh evil?"

Throughout his presentation, Barker remained focused on rationalist foundations, rejecting the epistemic validity of revelation, scripture, or spiritual experience. He claimed that such sources are unverifiable and often internally contradictory. Instead, he insisted that beliefs should be proportionate to the evidence available, and that extraordinary claims—such as the existence of a supernatural creator—require extraordinary evidence.

In contrast, Hassanain Rajabali's opening argument approached the question of God's existence from a metaphysical and theological perspective rooted in Islamic philosophy. Rather than engaging on purely empirical terms, Rajabali argued for the necessity of a transcendent being as the source of all existence. "There is no effect without a cause," he asserted, "and the universe, with all its complexity, cannot be the product of nothing." For Rajabali, existence itself is a sign (*āyah*) that points to a Necessary Existent (*wājib al-wujūd*), one who is self-sufficient, absolute, and uncaused.

A central theme in Rajabali's opening remarks was the distinction between absolute and relative existence. He contended that human logic, while effective in navigating empirical phenomena, is inherently limited when applied to metaphysical realities. "God," he stated, "is not part of the created world and thus cannot be subject to its laws or its forms of reasoning." This foundational distinction allowed Rajabali to defend the coherence of divine attributes that might appear paradoxical when viewed through a strictly materialist lens.

Rajabali also addressed the design and purpose evident in nature, citing examples such as the fine-tuning of the universe and the intricate design of biological life. He challenged the assumption that such precision could emerge from random processes, asserting that behind every order is an intention. "Chance," he said, "does not produce order on this scale. When we see signs of purpose, we infer a purposeful agent." This line of argument echoed classical teleological reasoning, reframed within a Qur'anic cosmology that views the universe as a purposeful, guided system.

On the question of morality, Rajabali offered a critique of relativism and argued that objective moral values cannot exist without a transcendent moral source. He posed the rhetorical question: "If morality is only a product of social consensus or evolution, then what makes murder, oppression, or deceit objectively wrong?" In contrast, he presented theism—and Islam in particular—as a coherent system that grounds morality in the immutable attributes of God, such as justice ('adl) and mercy (raḥmah).

In response to Barker's Problem of Evil, Rajabali offered the Islamic perspective that life is a test and that suffering has spiritual value. "Evil," he argued, "is not a thing in itself but the absence of good. Trials refine the soul and build moral character." Drawing from Qur'anic verses, he emphasized that God's justice is absolute, but human perception of justice is often limited by ignorance of the ultimate outcomes.

Rajabali concluded his remarks by appealing to the human experience of spirituality, love, awe, and conscience—phenomena which, he argued, cannot be fully explained by material causes. For him, these dimensions of human life point to a deeper reality, a Creator who is nearer than one's jugular vein (Qur'an 50:16), and who invites all people to seek Him through reason, reflection, and sincerity.

Hassanain Rajabali's Rebuttal

In his rebuttal to Dan Barker's opening presentation, Hassanain

Rajabali addressed the foundational assumptions and logical structure of Barker's atheism. Rather than offering a line-by-line refutation, Rajabali engaged with the overarching framework of Barker's argument, questioning its epistemological consistency, moral implications, and metaphysical depth.

Challenging Empiricism as the Sole Path to Truth:

Rajabali began by questioning Barker's reliance on empiricism as the only valid method for acquiring knowledge. He pointed out that while empirical methods are suitable for the natural sciences, they are inadequate for probing existential and metaphysical questions—such as the origin of existence, consciousness, or morality. "The assumption that only what is empirically verifiable is true," he argued, "is itself not empirically verifiable." This self-referential problem, Rajabali noted, undermines the epistemological foundation of strict empiricism.

He highlighted how much of what is meaningful in human life—such as love, justice, and purpose—cannot be quantified or measured, yet they remain undeniable aspects of our lived reality. By reducing truth to what is observable, Barker's worldview, according to Rajabali, not only limits the scope of inquiry but also dismisses a vast dimension of human experience.

On the Free Will Argument (FANG):

Rajabali directly engaged Barker's Free Will Argument for the Non-Existence of God (FANG), in which Barker claimed that divine foreknowledge is incompatible with human freedom. Rajabali responded by reframing the issue within a metaphysical understanding of time and divine knowledge. He argued that God's knowledge is not linear or anticipatory but timeless. God does not "predict" future events; He knows them in a single, eternal act of knowledge that does not interfere with human choice.

"Knowledge does not cause the act," Rajabali stated. "Just because God knows what you will choose does not mean He forces you to choose it." He illustrated this point with the example of a teacher who knows a student will fail an exam due to prior performance. The teacher's foreknowledge does not negate the student's freedom to perform. Thus, divine omniscience and human free will are not mutually exclusive, provided one understands God's knowledge as transcending time.

On the Problem of Evil:

In addressing Barker's invocation of the Problem of Evil, Rajabali acknowledged the emotional and philosophical weight of the issue but cautioned against simplistic conclusions. He noted that suffering is an inevitable part of human life and that its existence does not contradict divine mercy or justice when seen through the lens of purpose and trial.

He explained the Islamic view that life is a temporary and purposeful test, designed to cultivate moral and spiritual growth. Evil, he asserted, is not an independently created entity but a consequence of human free will and a necessary contrast through which good becomes meaningful. "Would courage have any value if there were no danger? Would compassion have any meaning without pain?" he asked rhetorically. For Rajabali, such experiences refine the soul and prepare it for an eternal life of proximity to God.

He also rejected the idea that God's non-intervention in every moment of suffering indicates absence or cruelty. Drawing from Qur'anic philosophy, he argued that God's mercy often operates through hidden wisdom, which may not be immediately comprehensible to human beings. "We must not conflate our limited understanding of fairness with divine justice," he asserted.

On Morality and Meaning:

Rajabali also took aim at Barker's secular moral framework, arguing that without an objective reference point, morality becomes a fluid and culturally conditioned construct. "If there is no God, then there is no accountability beyond societal opinion," he claimed. He warned that such relativism undermines the moral force behind concepts like justice, human rights, and dignity.

He posed a powerful rhetorical question: "If society declared murder acceptable, would it become moral?" For Rajabali, the mere existence of a conscience and the widespread human intuition of right and wrong point to an innate awareness of divine law (fitrah). He contrasted this with Barker's utilitarian approach, which, while pragmatic, lacks transcendent grounding.

Concluding Remarks in the Rebuttal:

Rajabali concluded his rebuttal by asserting that atheism, as presented by Barker, fails to account for the deeper questions of existence, purpose, and value. He invited the audience to reflect not merely on whether God exists, but on what the denial of God implies for the human condition.

> "Our very need to ask why—our pursuit of truth, love, and justice—are signs that point beyond the material," he said. "They point to a Creator who is not distant, but nearer than our jugular vein."

Dan Barker's Rebuttal

Dan Barker's rebuttal to Hassanain Rajabali's theistic opening centered on contesting the presuppositions, coherence, and epistemological foundations of religious belief. With a tone of respectful disagreement, Barker challenged the philosophical and theological claims made by Rajabali, emphasizing the insufficiency of metaphysical reasoning and the superiority of empirical evidence in evaluating truth claims.

Challenging the Argument from Design:

Barker began his rebuttal by disputing the inference that complexity and apparent design in nature necessarily point to a designer.

While Rajabali had used examples like the intricacies of the human body and cosmic fine-tuning to suggest intentional creation, Barker countered that such arguments commit a fallacy of analogy. "Just because something appears designed," he argued, "does not mean it is designed." He pointed to Darwinian evolution, natural selection, and abiogenesis as natural explanations for complexity, noting that invoking God as a designer imposes a far more complex explanation than the phenomena themselves.

He continued, "To claim that complexity requires a designer is to postulate an even more complex being. Who designed the designer?" According to Barker, this results in an infinite regress unless one arbitrarily stops at God, which, he asserted, is a non-answer. He concluded that invoking a divine designer does not simplify the equation but complicates it without empirical support.

On the Cosmological Argument and the "First Cause":

Barker also addressed Rajabali's cosmological reasoning—namely, that everything that exists must have a cause, and thus the universe must have a necessary, uncaused cause (i.e., God). Barker rejected this framework on two grounds. First, he questioned the assumption that everything must have a cause, especially in light of quantum physics, where certain subatomic events appear to occur without deterministic causes. Second, he criticized the special pleading inherent in exempting God from the causal chain. "Why can God be uncaused, but not the universe?" he asked.

Instead of positing a metaphysical entity to explain existence, Barker suggested that the universe could simply be a brute fact—something that exists without need of explanation. "Not knowing something is not a license to insert a deity," he remarked, reiterating his central theme: absence of evidence is grounds for disbelief.

Rejection of Metaphysical Absolutes:

Barker was particularly critical of Rajabali's appeal to metaphysical absolutes. He viewed such claims as speculative and unfalsifiable. "Talking about 'absolute' and 'relative' existence might sound profound," he said, "but these are just word games unless they can be tested." Barker argued that religious language often dresses up ignorance in philosophical terminology. To him, arguments for a transcendent being lack practical or scientific coherence because they are not grounded in observable reality.

He also questioned the utility of theological claims that place God "outside of time and space." If God is entirely outside the realm of physical reality, he asked, then how can such a being interact with that reality or be meaningfully described? "To say God is beyond logic, time, and space," Barker argued, "is effectively to say He's beyond comprehension—and therefore beyond belief."

On Morality and the Source of Ethics:

Barker responded directly to Rajabali's assertion that atheists cannot ground objective morality. He argued that moral values do not require a divine lawgiver, but can emerge from human empathy, evolutionary social behavior, and reason. "Morality is about minimizing harm and promoting well-being," Barker explained. He pointed out that atheists, like theists, can and do live ethical lives—often motivated by compassion, not command.

To support his argument, Barker referenced examples from secular societies with high standards of living, low crime rates, and strong social cohesion—many of which are less religious. He suggested that tying morality to divine command theory introduces greater danger, as it may justify unethical behavior under the guise of religious obedience. "If morality is simply obedience to God," he posed, "then was Abraham moral when he prepared to kill his son?"[1]

---

[1] Obedience to God is not moral *because* it is blind or authoritarian—it is moral *because* God is all-wise, all-knowing, and just. In other words, His commands are not arbitrary; they are always aligned with what is objectively

He concluded that secular morality, while imperfect, has the advantage of being adaptable, reasoned, and based on shared human experiences, not dogmatic decrees.

On the Problem of Evil and Divine Justice:

Turning to the issue of suffering and divine justice, Barker argued that Rajabali's theodicy—life as a test—fails to justify the scale and apparent randomness of suffering in the world. He noted that if God is both loving and omnipotent, then creating a world with so much pain, disease, and injustice appears unnecessary, if not cruel.

"If an all-knowing God already knows who will pass or fail this 'test,' then why administer it at all?" Barker asked. He challenged the internal coherence of a divine test that seems to operate with real-world consequences—poverty, war, natural disasters—that often fall on the innocent. Such suffering, he asserted, is better explained as a byproduct of an indifferent universe rather than as part of a benevolent plan.

He also questioned the morality of eternal punishment for finite sins. "What kind of loving being would create a Hell for people who simply disbelieve due to lack of evidence?" he asked, arguing that eternal damnation is disproportionate and morally indefensible.

On Spiritual Experience and Subjectivity:

Rajabali had appealed to inner experiences—such as awe, love, and conscience—as evidence for the divine. Barker acknowledged the power of such feelings but warned against conflating emotion with truth. "People of all religions feel spiritual awe," he observed. "Does that make all their contradictory gods true?" He emphasized that subjective experience, while personally meaningful, is not a reliable guide for establishing objective facts.

---

wise and beneficial, even when not immediately comprehensible to human minds. (Ed.)

Conclusion of Barker's Rebuttal:

Dan Barker closed his rebuttal by reiterating that the burden of proof lies on the theist. He did not claim to have all the answers about the universe's origin or the source of morality. Instead, he emphasized intellectual honesty, skepticism, and the courage to say "I don't know" rather than appealing to unverifiable metaphysics.

> "We don't need a god to explain love. We don't need a god to explain morality. And we don't need a god to live meaningful lives," he concluded. "We just need reason, compassion, and the willingness to think for ourselves."

Q&A Session

Following the structured debate, a diverse set of written questions was submitted by audience members to both Dan Barker and Hassanain Rajabali. The Q&A session extended the conversation into more personal, moral, and theological territories, offering a clearer view of how each speaker applied their worldview to real-life concerns. Below is a thematic analysis of "key questions" raised and how each debater responded.

1. Morality Without God

Question: How can an atheist justify moral obligations without a divine lawgiver?

Dan Barker's Response: Barker reiterated his position that morality is a human phenomenon rooted in the intent to reduce harm and promote well-being. He explained that moral values arise from empathy, shared social contracts, evolutionary behavior, and the needs of cooperative societies. Referencing secular humanist ethics, he argued that moral reasoning does not require religious belief, citing examples of highly secular countries with low crime and high happiness indexes.

Hassanain Rajabali's Response: Rajabali challenged the sufficiency of Barker's framework, asserting that a morality grounded in empathy and societal consensus lacks objectivity and permanence. He questioned how certain acts—such as genocide or slavery—could be judged morally wrong if morality is subjective or culturally relative. Rajabali emphasized that belief in God anchors moral principles in an immutable source, ensuring that right and wrong are not dictated by majority opinion or personal preference.

Analysis: This exchange highlighted a foundational tension: Barker emphasized functional morality based on outcomes and human consensus, whereas Rajabali argued for principled morality rooted in divine authority. The question exposed the broader philosophical question of whether morality can be truly objective without metaphysical foundations.

2. Scientific Value of Prayer

Question: Is there any scientific evidence that prayer works?

Hassanain Rajabali's Response: Rajabali pointed to studies suggesting that prayer has psychosomatic and psychological benefits. He acknowledged that while the spiritual effects of prayer may not always be measurable through conventional methods, its impact on mental health, focus, and emotional regulation is significant. He also stressed that prayer is not merely transactional but relational—an act of aligning oneself with the divine.

Dan Barker's Response: Barker dismissed the notion that prayer has any supernatural efficacy. He cited studies—particularly those with double-blind, controlled methodologies—that failed to show any statistically significant correlation between intercessory prayer and medical outcomes. He conceded that personal prayer may have therapeutic or meditative benefits, but argued that such effects are indistinguishable from those produced by non-religious forms of mindfulness or reflection.

Analysis: This question allowed both speakers to affirm different functions of prayer: Rajabali emphasized spiritual alignment and metaphysical connectivity, while Barker focused on empirical verification. The contrast highlighted their broader views on what counts as legitimate evidence.

3. The Justice of Hell

Question: How can eternal punishment be justified for finite actions?

Dan Barker's Response: Barker sharply criticized the doctrine of Hell as morally indefensible. He argued that a loving and just being would not inflict eternal suffering for temporal disbelief or sin. According to him, Hell represents divine tyranny, especially when it punishes sincere non-believers who, in good faith, find no evidence for God. "Infinite punishment for finite misdeeds is not justice," he stated, "it's cruelty."

Hassanain Rajabali's Response: Rajabali explained the Islamic understanding of Hell as a consequence—not merely a punishment—of one's own choices and orientation toward truth. He described it as the metaphysical result of a soul that persistently rejects divine mercy and guidance. Hell, he noted, is not arbitrary but earned. Importantly, he emphasized that God's mercy far outweighs His wrath, and that the path to forgiveness remains open throughout life.

Analysis: This question unearthed contrasting views on divine justice: Barker viewed Hell through a humanistic lens as disproportionate and cruel, while Rajabali framed it within a theological context of free will, divine justice, and eschatological consequences.

4. The Agnostic Seeker's Dilemma

Question: Is it arrogant to claim certainty about God's existence or non-existence?

Hassanain Rajabali's Response: Rajabali welcomed the question's tone of humility and inquiry. He acknowledged the legitimacy of doubt when grounded in sincere seeking. Citing Qur'anic verses, he argued that the human soul is naturally inclined (fitrah) toward the divine and that God's signs are evident in creation, reason, and moral intuition. "Certainty comes not from arrogance," he said, "but from spiritual and intellectual awakening."

Dan Barker's Response: Barker responded that skepticism is a virtue, not a vice. He encouraged agnostics to continue questioning and to withhold belief until compelling evidence is found. He cautioned against mistaking subjective experiences or cultural conditioning for truth, and praised the questioner's honesty in admitting what they do not know.

Analysis: This exchange brought out the temperaments of both speakers: Rajabali's spiritual optimism and belief in innate guidance contrasted with Barker's epistemic caution and emphasis on critical thinking. Both validated the questioner's sincerity, though they diverged on where such a journey ought to lead.

5. Science, God, and the Gaps

Question: Does science not eventually fill the gaps religion tries to explain?

Dan Barker's Response: Barker reaffirmed his belief in the "God of the gaps" fallacy, criticizing religious explanations for leaning on ignorance. He suggested that as science progresses, the need for supernatural explanations diminishes. He argued that historically, phenomena once attributed to deities—like lightning or disease—are now understood through natural laws.

Hassanain Rajabali's Response: Rajabali responded that theism does not rely on gaps in knowledge but on positive metaphysical and moral reasoning. He argued that science can only describe how things work, not why they exist. He claimed that reductionist models fail to account for the origin of rationality, consciousness, or values. "Science is a method," he noted, "not a worldview. It needs a metaphysical foundation it cannot itself supply."

Analysis: This exchange highlighted an ongoing philosophical debate: whether science and religion address mutually exclusive domains, or whether one renders the other obsolete. Barker viewed science as replacing religion; Rajabali saw it as a tool that operates within a theistic framework.

Review Of Key Arguments

The Problem of Evil

Hassanain Rajabali's Response to the Problem of Evil: Suffering as a Test, Not a Contradiction

When confronted with the classic Problem of Evil—how an all-powerful, all-knowing, and all-merciful God could allow pain, injustice, and suffering—Hassanain Rajabali offered a deeply theological and philosophical response grounded in Islamic metaphysics, moral psychology, and a teleological view of human life.

Rather than seeing evil and suffering as contradictions to divine goodness, Rajabali presented them as integral components of a purposeful and morally developmental universe. He argued that what we call "evil" often reflects a limited and short-term human perception, rather than a comprehensive understanding of divine wisdom.

Key Elements of Rajabali's Response

1. Life is a Test

Rajabali repeatedly emphasized that this world is a testing ground, a place where human beings are given the opportunity to exercise free will, develop moral character, and move toward spiritual perfection. Suffering, challenges, and even tragedy are not signs of divine absence or indifference, but of purposeful trial.

> "Would there be valor if there were no danger? Would there be compassion if there were no pain? Would there be generosity without need?"

He used educational metaphors to illustrate this point, likening life to a school. Just as a student must undergo tests and confront difficult material to mature intellectually, the human soul must undergo moral and spiritual trials to actualize its potential. Evil, in this context, serves a functional role—as a contrast to good, as a catalyst for moral action, and as an instrument of growth.

2. Evil is Relative, Not Absolute

Rajabali framed evil not as a created entity but as a privation of good—similar to how darkness is the absence of light or cold is the absence of heat. He argued that evil does not exist independently, but emerges from the misuse of free will or the absence of good in certain situations.

> "God did not create evil as a substance. He created the possibility of choice, and with that comes the risk of wrong decisions."

This metaphysical understanding of evil absolves God of moral wrongdoing while preserving human responsibility. It also highlights that much of what we call evil—such as greed, violence, and injustice—is man-made and the result of human choices, not divine intervention.

3. Examples from the Natural and Human World

Rajabali offered or implied several examples to reinforce his perspective:

Pain in the body: He explained that pain is not an evil per se, but a necessary signal for survival. Without pain, we wouldn't know when to remove our hand from fire or seek treatment for illness.

Sickness and disease: While tragic, these serve as reminders of human vulnerability, leading to compassion, humility, and even breakthroughs in medicine and community care.

Death and bereavement: Rather than viewing death as an evil, Rajabali placed it within a divine context of transience and transition, where the soul moves on to a more complete form of life in the Hereafter.

Injustice in the world (e.g., war, oppression): He argued that these are the consequences of human greed, pride, and negligence—not God's will. However, the victims of such injustices are not forgotten by God; they are rewarded in the Hereafter, and divine justice will ultimately prevail.

4. The Greater Good and Divine Wisdom

Rajabali acknowledged that human beings often cannot perceive the long-term or hidden benefits that may arise from suffering. Drawing on Qur'anic principles, he cited verses like:

> "Perhaps you dislike something while it is good for you, and perhaps you like something while it is bad for you; and Allah knows, while you do not know." (2:216)

He insisted that God's wisdom encompasses layers of reality inaccessible to human reason. Just as a child cannot understand why a loving parent denies them something or disciplines them, we too may misinterpret divine actions due to epistemic limitation.

5. Divine Mercy Prevails

Rajabali reminded the audience that in Islam, God's mercy overrides His wrath. He referenced the Hadith that says: "My mercy prevails over My wrath." Even within suffering, there are countless signs of mercy—acts of human kindness, resilience, communal solidarity, and the opportunity for reflection and change.

> "Even when we cry, it is the mercy of God that gives us the capacity to feel and to hope."

Conclusion: Suffering as a Path to God

In sum, Rajabali's answer to the Problem of Evil was neither a denial of pain nor a dismissal of the emotional and ethical gravity of suffering. Rather, he recontextualized suffering as a means of soul-building, a function of free will, and a part of a grander, divinely-willed process of moral development. Evil, he contended, is real—but not incompatible with God's existence. In fact, it is the very existence of evil that calls us toward justice, compassion, and ultimately, toward God.

Can God Be Both All-Merciful and All-Just?

Dan Barker's Argument: The Logical Discrepancy Between Mercy and Justice

During the debate, Dan Barker presented a focused critique on the coherence of divine attributes—specifically the claim that God is simultaneously all-Merciful (*al-Raḥmān, al-Raḥīm*) and all-Just (*al-ʿAdl*). Barker contended that these two traits, when taken to their logical extremes, are mutually exclusive.

He explained that justice, by definition, requires giving each person exactly what they deserve. Mercy, on the other hand, involves withholding punishment or granting leniency in cases where it is deserved. Thus, a truly merciful act is, in essence, a suspension or alteration of justice. For example, a judge who pardons a guilty criminal is not being just in that moment; they are being merciful—but at the cost of strict justice. Barker argued:

> "If God is merciful and forgives, then He is not giving people what they deserve. But if He is just, and gives them exactly what they deserve, then He is not being merciful. You can't have it both ways."

Barker used this tension to critique the internal coherence of divine nature in Abrahamic theology. He further questioned how an omniscient and omnipotent deity could create beings knowing they would fail, and still claim to be just by condemning them eternally. In his view, the doctrine of Hell, especially for finite earthly sins or disbelief, contradicts both divine justice (disproportionality) and divine mercy (lack of compassion).

Hassanain Rajabali's Response: Divine Justice and Mercy as Complementary, Not Contradictory

Rajabali responded to this critique by asserting that divine attributes are not compartmentalized like human traits. In Islamic theology, God's names and attributes exist in perfect harmony, not contradiction. What appears to be a paradox from a human perspective, he argued, is a product of limited reasoning applied to an infinite and absolute reality.

He explained that divine justice and mercy operate on different levels:

Justice ('*Adl*) ensures that every action has a consequence—good is rewarded, and wrongdoing does not go unaddressed.

Mercy (Raḥmah) functions as a higher-order reality, offering forgiveness, elevation, and grace beyond what is deserved. Rajabali said:

> "God is just to those who demand it—and merciful to those who seek it," "His mercy does not negate His justice, but transcends it."

He further clarified that in the Islamic worldview, divine mercy is the default: God wants to forgive and uplift. The Qur'an repeatedly affirms: "My mercy encompasses all things" (Qur'an 7:156). Punishment, on the other hand, is reserved for those who knowingly reject truth, violate others, and refuse repentance.

To address the courtroom analogy, Rajabali reframed the role of God not as a mechanical judge, but as a loving Creator who understands the context of every individual's life, intentions, and struggles. Thus, divine judgment takes into account not only the deed, but the internal state and circumstances of the person.

> "Mercy is not the absence of justice," he emphasized, "but its perfect fulfillment when delivered by One who knows all dimensions of a soul."

He offered the example of a repentant sinner: God's justice would demand accountability, but His mercy—invoked through sincere remorse, transformation, and good deeds—would override punishment, not ignore it. This, in Rajabali's view, is not a contradiction but a superior moral paradigm, where justice exists not as mechanical retribution, but as part of a nurturing divine plan.

Theological and Philosophical Implications

The tension raised by Barker taps into a longstanding debate in the philosophy of religion. But while human systems often treat justice and mercy as opposites, Islamic theology (and classical theism more broadly) posits a God who embodies these traits in a non-conflicting unity. In this view, God's knowledge of every detail—including intention, history, capacity, and repentance—allows Him to justly apply mercy.

Barker's critique reflects a secular legalistic understanding, where justice is punitive and mercy is discretionary. Rajabali's response draws from theological ethics, where justice and mercy are calibrated by divine wisdom, not fixed codes.

Summary of the Exchange

Barker argued that mercy and justice, if taken as absolutes, logically cancel each other out. If God is always just, He must punish. If He is always merciful, He must forgive. Therefore, He cannot be both at the same time.

Rajabali responded that divine justice is holistic and fully informed, unlike human justice. Mercy, in the divine sense, is an expression of justice that restores, reforms, and elevates rather than simply pardoning arbitrarily. Thus, God can be both perfectly just and perfectly merciful, because He judges in perfect knowledge and compassion.

Can God's Existence Be Tested?

Dan Barker's Argument: The Problem of Unfalsifiability

Dan Barker invoked the principle of falsifiability as a key critique of theistic claims. In essence, this principle holds that for a proposition to be considered scientific or meaningful in a truth-claiming sense, it must be falsifiable—that is, it must be possible to conceive of evidence that could prove it wrong. Barker argued:

> "If you can't tell me what would falsify your claim, then you're not making a claim about reality; you're making a statement of belief or emotion."

He asserted that God, as commonly defined by theists—immaterial, timeless, beyond nature, and outside empirical detection—is unfalsifiable by design. Any attempt to test or verify God's existence is deflected by the assertion that God is "beyond the senses," "beyond logic," or "not subject to empirical constraints." Barker maintained that such a definition removes God from the realm of investigable reality, making the claim immune to challenge—and thus, philosophically and scientifically meaningless as a truth proposition.

For Barker, this places God in the same category as unfalsifiable ideas such as:

» The Flying Spaghetti Monster

» Invisible pink unicorns

» Russell's teapot orbiting the Sun

He argued that if we accept unfalsifiable claims as valid without evidence, then we must accept all such claims equally. Therefore, to distinguish true beliefs from false ones, we must hold ideas accountable to empirical testing, logical coherence, and falsifiability.

Hassanain Rajabali's Response: Metaphysics and the Limits of Empiricism

Rajabali did not reject the value of falsifiability in science, but he challenged its application to metaphysical and ontological questions, such as the existence of God. He argued that not all truths are empirical or testable in a laboratory, yet they are no less real or meaningful. Rajabali countered:

> "Falsifiability is a useful scientific method—but it is not the only path to truth," "Love is not falsifiable. Purpose is not falsifiable. Yet we live by them."

He contended that reality is broader than what science can measure, and that God, as a metaphysical reality, transcends the material tools of falsification. Just as one does not use a thermometer to measure justice or a microscope to examine beauty, God's existence must be approached through rational reflection, moral experience, and spiritual intuition—not through the lens of laboratory science.

Rajabali also warned of the dangers of scientism—the view that science is the only legitimate source of knowledge. He pointed out that this position is self-defeating, because the claim "only science can give us truth" is itself not a scientific statement, but a philosophical one.

He further argued that many foundational beliefs are not falsifiable, yet they are essential:

» The belief that human beings have intrinsic value

» The existence of free will

» The reality of consciousness

» The immutability of logical laws

These, like belief in God, are not empirically falsifiable, yet they underpin much of human thought and civilization.

An Essay on the Principle of Falsifiability

In the debate, Dan Barker sought to undermine the coherence of theism by invoking the principle of falsifiability. He argued that the God hypothesis fails the test of rational credibility because it is unfalsifiable—that is, there is no conceivable condition under which God's nonexistence could be demonstrated. To many in the audience unfamiliar with the philosophical limits of this principle, Barker's challenge may have sounded decisive. Yet a closer examination reveals that the appeal to falsifiability, while appropriate in scientific contexts, becomes problematic—and indeed philosophically misguided—when applied to metaphysical realities.

This essay argues that Barker's use of the falsifiability principle to critique belief in God constitutes a category error: he applies a test developed for empirical hypotheses to a domain that transcends empirical observation. The result is not a meaningful refutation of theism, but a confusion of epistemological categories.

Falsifiability was introduced by Karl Popper and Rudolf Carnap in the 1930s as a demarcation criterion to distinguish scientific theories from non-scientific ones. According to Popper, a proposition is scientific if and only if it is capable of being tested and, potentially, proven false by empirical observation. For example:

The claim "Water boils at 100°C at sea level" is falsifiable because it can be tested.

The claim "A teapot is orbiting the sun somewhere between Earth and Mars, but it's too small to detect" is unfalsifiable and therefore unscientific.

Popper did not argue that unfalsifiable claims are meaningless—only that they fall outside the domain of science.[1]

---

[1] Popper associated falsifiability with empirical claims, arguing that metaphysical or philosophical assertions are, by their nature, not subject to falsification. He further distinguished between empirical statements that are inherently untestable—termed "pure existential statements"—and

During the debate, Dan Barker challenged Hassanain Rajabali by pointing out that the theistic concept of God is immune to disproof:

> "You're saying nothing can ever count as evidence against your belief. That's not reason—that's dogma."

In essence, Barker argued that because no experiment or observation could ever disprove the existence of God, belief in God is irrational or unscientific. He portrayed this as a failure of theism to meet the standards of critical inquiry and epistemic responsibility.

However, this move—though rhetorically forceful—commits a category mistake. It assumes that metaphysical truths ought to be evaluated by the standards of empirical science, a view not shared by most philosophers, including many atheists.

The Limits of Falsifiability in Metaphysics:

Metaphysical claims are not empirical claims. They are a priori (known through reason and logic) rather than a posteriori (known through sensory observation). As such, they belong to a different epistemic domain than propositions in physics, chemistry, or biology.

Examples of metaphysical principles include:

» The law of non-contradiction

» The principle of sufficient reason

» The claim that something cannot come from nothing

» The claim that contingent beings require a necessary cause

---

those that are limited in scope and therefore potentially falsifiable, which he referred to as "restricted" existential statements. (Ed.)

None of these are falsifiable in the Popperian sense—but they are still rationally defensible and philosophically significant. To dismiss them because they are not testable is to ignore the very foundations of coherent thought.[1]

Similarly, the claim "God exists as a necessary being" is not an empirical hypothesis; it is a metaphysical explanation for why contingent reality exists at all. It is evaluated not through experimentation, but through logical coherence, explanatory power, and philosophical necessity.

Victor J. Stenger writes in his book *God - The Failed Hypothesis* (2013):

> By this criterion, it would seem that the existence of God cannot be empirically refuted because to do so would require making an existential statement applying to the whole universe (plus whatever lies beyond). But, in looking at Popper's example, we see this is not the case for God. True, we cannot refute the existence of a God who, like the pearl in Popper's example, is somewhere outside the box, say, in another galaxy. But God is supposed to be everywhere, including inside every box. So when we search for God inside a single box, no matter how small, we should either find him, thus confirming his existence, or not find him, thus refuting his existence.

The primary flaw in Victor's argument is a misclassification: it assumes that God's omnipresence is akin to physical presence. That is, if something is "everywhere," then it must be materially detectable. But in Islamic theology—especially as articulated in the Qur'an and further refined by classical theologians such as Imam al-Ghazālī, Mulla Ṣadrā, and Allāmah Ṭabāṭabā'ī—God's presence is not spatial or material.

---

[1] In scientific practice, theories that initially fail empirical tests are frequently adjusted to accommodate the data. Although some philosophers argue that this undermines the concept of falsification, such adjustments typically result in a revised model, while the original version remains considered falsified. (Ed.)

Qur'an (6:103): "Vision perceives Him not, but He perceives [all] vision; and He is the Subtle, the All-Aware."

Qur'an (57:4): "He is with you wherever you are."

Here, the *ma'iyyah* (with-ness) of God is not physical co-location but existential sustenance—He is with His creation not by spatial nearness, but through His active sustaining of their being. To assume that God's presence must be empirically observable is to anthropomorphize the divine, reducing transcendence to immanence.

Islamic theology distinguishes between God's essence (dhāt) and His attributes and effects (āthār). When we say God is everywhere, we mean He is present in terms of His knowledge, power, authority, and creative act—not in His essence. Imam 'Alī (a.s.) said:

> "He is with everything, not through mingling, and distinct from everything, not through separation."[1]

Thus, the statement "God is in the box" is misleading if understood materially. The correct expression is that God sustains the box, knows what is in the box, and has authority over the box—not that His essence is physically in it.

How did Rajabali respond to Barker?

He responded to Barker's challenge by shifting the focus from scientific verification to metaphysical reasoning. He argued that the universe—being relative, finite, and contingent—could not exist without a necessary cause:

> "You are asking a question which is really an impossibility by its own nature. If you say that there is a reasonable answer for no creator... that answer must still be God, whether or not you call it that."

---

[1] *Nahj al-Balāghah*, Sermon 1

Far from evading falsifiability, Rajabali questioned why falsifiability should be the gold standard in the first place. He pushed the audience to ask whether science is equipped to answer questions like:

Why is there something rather than nothing?

What grounds the very possibility of existence?

What accounts for intelligibility, order, and consciousness?

In doing so, Rajabali exposed the limitation of Barker's criteria: science can explain how things happen, but it cannot explain why there is anything to explain in the first place. To demand that God be falsifiable is to demand that the ultimate metaphysical ground of reality be subjected to the standards of empirical phenomena—a contradiction in terms.

Why Falsifiability Doesn't Apply

There are at least three strong reasons why falsifiability cannot be coherently applied to the God question:

a. Category Difference: God, as conceived in classical theism, is not a physical entity subject to observation. God is the necessary ground of all being—not one being among others. To look for God with a telescope or a lab test is to misdefine the nature of the claim itself.

b. Philosophical Necessity, Not Scientific Hypothesis: The existence of God is argued from logical necessity (e.g., contingency, morality, consciousness), not from testable predictions. It is more akin to the validity of logic or the existence of minds—things that are rationally inferred, not empirically measured.

c. Misuse of Scientific Tools: Falsifiability is designed for natural sciences—not metaphysical or ethical reasoning. To use it against theism is like trying to weigh justice with a thermometer or analyze love with a microscope. The tool is simply not suited to the task.

Conclusion:

Dan Barker's use of falsifiability to dismiss the God hypothesis may resonate with audiences accustomed to scientific reasoning, but it fails as a philosophical objection. It conflates two distinct domains of thought—science and metaphysics—and uses a tool appropriate to one to improperly judge the other.

Hassanain Rajabali, by contrast, invites a deeper inquiry into the preconditions of reason, existence, and morality. His argument is not about filling gaps in scientific knowledge with "God"—it is about understanding that even science itself rests on metaphysical assumptions that point beyond themselves.

The principle of falsifiability, powerful though it is, must remain within its proper bounds. When misapplied to ultimate metaphysical questions, it does not expose weakness in theism—it reveals the limits of empiricism.

Morality Without God?

Among the most philosophically charged moments in the debate was the recurring argument over morality. Beyond questions of cosmology, design, or divine revelation, morality presents an inescapably human concern. It is not only about the metaphysical question of whether moral values are real, but the existential question of why we should care about being good at all. This segment of the debate revealed profound disagreements—not merely about right and wrong—but about the very nature and foundation of ethics.

Morality and the Question of God:

Hassanain Rajabali, representing the theistic perspective, advanced a moral argument rooted in divine accountability. For him, the presence of an objective moral order presupposes the existence of a moral Lawgiver—namely, God. Without God, he contended, morality would be reduced to subjective opinion, cultural convention, or utilitarian convenience. His argument was not merely about behavior, but about why human beings are obliged to act morally in the first place.

Rajabali articulated this point clearly:

> "Without God, what makes anything truly right or wrong? What stops someone from committing evil if they think they can get away with it?"

He reinforced this position by citing examples of historical moral atrocities—such as those perpetrated by Hitler or Stalin—arguing that without a higher moral standard, such actions cannot be definitively condemned. His conclusion: only belief in a moral God provides a binding, objective foundation for ethical conduct.

In contrast, Dan Barker, arguing from a secular humanist standpoint, insisted that morality is not contingent on belief in God. As a former evangelical preacher turned atheist, Barker brought personal experience to his case, stating that he leads a moral life not out of fear of divine punishment, but from empathy, reason, and a commitment to human well-being. He argued that morality arises from our shared human nature and social interdependence:

> "Morality comes from empathy, reason, and shared human experience. We are social beings."

Barker rejected the premise that atheism leads to moral nihilism. He offered examples of secular societies with high ethical standards and pointed out that moral behavior predates religion. In doing so, he sought to demonstrate that one can be good without God—a central tenet of modern secular ethics.

The Ontological Disagreement: What Morality Is

At the heart of the disagreement lies a meta-ethical divide. Rajabali was concerned with moral ontology: what grounds the existence of moral truths. For him, values like justice, kindness, and honesty cannot merely be human inventions. They must exist independently of us, as reflections of divine will. Without such grounding, he argued, there is no objective way to say that one action is truly better than another.

Barker, on the other hand, focused on moral epistemology and practice: how we know what is right and how we live morally. He argued that evolution has equipped us with moral instincts and that societies develop ethical systems to minimize harm and foster cooperation. For Barker, we don't need a divine legislator to recognize the value of kindness or the wrongness of murder.

However, the debate revealed that neither side fully addressed the other's framework. Rajabali did not acknowledge that secular moral philosophies can and do offer serious accounts of moral objectivity—such as moral realism or contractualism. Likewise, Barker did not engage directly with the challenge of normativity—that is, explaining why someone should follow a moral rule if they do not feel like it or if it contradicts their interests.

Accountability and Fear:

One of the more controversial parts of the exchange was Rajabali's claim that atheists lack ultimate accountability, which makes their moral framework unreliable. He suggested that if someone believes they can commit evil without consequence, then nothing compels them to choose good. This argument was rhetorically powerful, especially with a religious audience, but it faced a philosophical objection.

Barker countered that doing good because of fear of punishment is not moral virtue but self-interest. He insisted that moral actions should come from genuine concern for others, not from coercion or divine threat. This line of critique challenges not only Islamic theology but also a broader theistic tradition that links moral action to reward and punishment in the afterlife.

However, Barker's counter did not fully dismantle Rajabali's central claim: that secular ethics struggles to explain ultimate moral obligation. While empathy and reason are powerful guides, they can vary. Not everyone is empathetic. Not every culture agrees on what constitutes harm. Rajabali seized upon this point to reiterate the need for a higher, unchanging standard.

Audience Reflections and the Power of Perception:

The audience Q&A session further exposed the deep concern many attendees had about moral collapse without religion. Several questions asked directly whether atheism could produce a sustainable, just society. Rajabali used these opportunities to underscore the importance of divine law in shaping behavior, while Barker attempted to reassure the audience that secularism does not mean moral anarchy.

Yet, as some reviewers noted, Barker could have been more effective in presenting a robust moral theory. He mentioned his ethical commitments but did not explain why they should be binding on others, especially those who do not share his values. In contrast, Rajabali's arguments resonated with those who believe morality must be more than consensus or sentiment.

Key Takeaways:

1. Two Frameworks, Different Questions: Rajabali focused on the foundation of moral values; Barker on their function. Both assumed different starting points, which led to mutual incomprehension at times.

2. Emotion and Ethics: Rajabali's argument had emotional and rhetorical weight, especially in a post-9/11 setting where religious identity and moral boundaries were under public scrutiny. Barker's calm, rational tone, while sincere, at times lacked emotive power.

3. Philosophical Depth vs. Audience Appeal: Rajabali appealed to the need for moral certainty and accountability—concepts that play well in public debates. Barker's emphasis on individual conscience and harm minimization appealed more to philosophical secularism

but required deeper exposition to convince skeptics.

4. Normativity Left Unanswered: One of the strongest critiques of Barker's position is that he did not fully confront the question: Why should we be moral at all? Without a compelling answer, secular morality can appear as contingent, optional, or culturally bound—precisely the weaknesses Rajabali sought to highlight.

5. Good Without God vs. Good Grounded in God: The debate reaffirmed a core divide in modern ethical philosophy. Theists argue that goodness must have a source beyond human beings. Secularists argue that being good does not require belief in that source. The clash lies not in the desire to be moral, but in the justification for morality.

Conclusion:

The morality argument in the Barker—Rajabali debate brought into sharp relief the deep metaphysical and existential tensions between theism and atheism. While Barker successfully demonstrated that atheists can and do live moral lives, Rajabali's challenge remained: What ultimately grounds your moral code, and why should it apply to everyone?

This segment of the debate is thus more than a philosophical exercise. It is a mirror for the broader cultural conflict over whether ethics can survive the retreat of religion, and whether meaning and obligation can flourish without transcendence. For readers on either side of the spectrum, the discussion offers not closure, but a deepened understanding of what's really at stake when we ask: What makes something right or wrong?

The Argument from the Universe

One of the central threads running through Hassanain Rajabali's defense of theism in his debate with Dan Barker was what can best be described as the Argument from the Universe. This macro-argument—though not labeled as such by Rajabali himself—was a composite of multiple classical theistic arguments, including the Ontological, Cosmological, and Design arguments. Rather than formally separating these lines of reasoning, Rajabali blended them into a singular metaphysical case for the necessity of God's existence. Dan Barker attempted to respond to this strategy, but the conflation of arguments created a philosophical tangle that was not easily unraveled within the time constraints of the debate.

The Architecture of Rajabali's Argument:

Rajabali's approach to the question "Does God Not Exist?" relied on what might be termed Evidential Presuppositionalism. While traditional presuppositional arguments assert that God must exist as the precondition for knowledge and rationality (usually an a priori claim), Rajabali inverted this by treating the empirical fact of the universe's existence as the starting point for a presuppositional claim. In other words, he argued that the universe is so finely ordered, so deeply imbued with design, and so dependent on cause, that it could not possibly exist without God.

He stated:

> "Everything around us—from the precise laws of physics to the consciousness within ourselves—points to a greater intelligence, a necessary being."

Rather than segment his argument into discrete categories, Rajabali wove together elements of:

The Ontological Argument – By implication, arguing that some being must necessarily exist to account for contingent existence.

The Cosmological Argument – That the universe cannot be self-originating; it must have a First Cause.

The Argument from Design (Teleological) – That the order, beauty, and complexity of the universe indicate purpose, intelligence, and design.

His rhetorical style emphasized certainty rather than speculation. He declared that God's existence is not merely a belief but a rational inevitability, a necessity implied by the very fact that something exists rather than nothing.

Dan Barker's Counterargument:

Dan Barker responded to this conglomerate position with a naturalistic counter-thesis. He acknowledged that the universe is vast, complex, and awe-inspiring, but denied that these features necessitate a divine cause. In doing so, he leaned on standard critiques of each of the classical arguments, though not always by name or in formal structure.

His rebuttals included:

To the Cosmological Line: If something must be uncaused or necessary, why not the universe itself? Why assume a conscious God as the First Cause rather than a non-personal foundation?

> "You claim God is necessary—but why can't the universe be necessary?"

To the Design Argument: Complexity does not necessarily imply design. Natural processes, governed by physical laws, can produce astonishing complexity without intelligent guidance.

> "Complexity can emerge from simple rules, as we see in nature."

To the Ontological Assumptions: While not directly addressed, Barker implied that the notion of a necessary being is not self-evident and that the universe, in principle, could be all that exists without invoking something supernatural.

Barker's overarching strategy was to resist inference to the best explanation when that explanation is God. Instead, he emphasized epistemic humility, proposing that ignorance or current gaps in scientific knowledge are not licenses for theistic inference.

> "Invoking God doesn't explain the universe—it just pushes the question back. Who created God?"

Key Takeaways:

1. Rajabali's Argument Was More Persuasive Than Precise

By merging multiple arguments into a single narrative about the universe requiring God, Rajabali created a sense of overwhelming plausibility—but at the cost of precision. Philosophically, each argument deserves separate treatment and analysis.

2. Barker's Strength Was Skepticism, But Not Construction

Barker was effective in poking holes in theistic arguments but was less successful in presenting a robust alternative metaphysics. His claim that the universe might be necessary or that complexity can arise naturally needed elaboration to carry equal weight.

3. The Debate Highlighted Theism's Narrative Power

Rajabali's argument appealed not only to logic but to existential longing—the desire for meaning, purpose, and intelligibility. Even if the argument was philosophically imperfect, it resonated emotionally and intuitively, particularly in a religious setting.

4. Scientific Gaps vs. Theological Assumptions

Barker tried to highlight the danger of "God-of-the-gaps" reasoning, while Rajabali asserted that God is not a gap filler but the foundation. This tension—between explanatory sufficiency and epistemic closure—remains central to all cosmological reasoning.

Conclusion:

The "Argument from the Universe" as articulated by Hassanain Rajabali stands out in the debate not because of its formal philosophical precision, but because of its cumulative force. By weaving together the Ontological, Cosmological, and Design arguments into a single evidential narrative, Rajabali presented the existence of the universe as not merely a phenomenon to be studied, but as a signpost pointing beyond itself. The order, intelligibility, and purpose observed in the cosmos were not treated as coincidental or brute facts, but as rational indicators of a necessary, intelligent, and purposeful Creator.

Though critics might argue that conflating these arguments sacrifices clarity, the strength of Rajabali's method lay in its coherence with lived human experience. The intuitive conviction that something does not come from nothing, that design implies a designer, and that the finely-tuned parameters of the universe are best explained by intention rather than chance—these resonate not only with the religious but with anyone attuned to meaning beyond mechanics.

Dan Barker's counterpoints, though logically valid in challenging the leap from universe to God, ultimately rested on philosophical minimalism—a readiness to accept the universe as a self-sufficient and unexplained fact. This is intellectually consistent but existentially dissatisfying for many. His reluctance to offer a positive metaphysical account, and his dependence on the limits of scientific explanation, left a noticeable void in terms of providing a comprehensive worldview.

In contrast, Rajabali's argument—anchored in the conviction that God is not merely an explanation, but the foundation of all existence—provided a more compelling and meaningful alternative. It reminded the audience that belief in God is not about inserting a deity into gaps of knowledge, but about recognizing that the very intelligibility of the universe, and our place within it, cries out for a transcendent source.

Thus, while both debaters approached the universe with different assumptions and aims, the theistic framework offered by Rajabali provided not only a rational but also a deeply coherent and purpose-oriented interpretation of reality—one that affirms the human longing for meaning, grounded not in speculation, but in the very structure of the cosmos.

The "God of the Gaps" Argument

One of the most common objections raised by contemporary atheists against arguments for the existence of God is the so-called "God of the Gaps" argument. The charge is that theists insert God into areas of scientific or philosophical ignorance—wherever there's a gap in knowledge, God is used as a placeholder. During the Does God Not Exist? debate, Dan Barker repeatedly leaned on this line of critique to dismiss theistic arguments as little more than appeals to ignorance.

Barker stated early in his remarks:

> "Many of these arguments are basically just 'God of the gaps.' They are arguments from his ignorance."

He reinforced this view later by citing Isaac Newton's appeal to divine causality in the absence of known physical laws governing the solar system, claiming:

> "He had a gap in his understanding; he plugged it with his god. And that's basically how the arguments for the existence of god have all boiled down."

However, as Hassanain Rajabali pointed out in his rebuttal, this objection rests on a category error and a misreading of the nature and intent of classical theistic reasoning. Rather than appealing to ignorance, Rajabali consistently rooted his argument in positive metaphysical inferences drawn from what we do know, not from what we don't.

Rajabali responded pointedly:

> "For you to say the idea of gaps, the god of the gaps, for you also to

say that there is no god is also a gap. I think your gap is much wider because for one to say, because of this incredible design, therefore there is no maker, no designer..."

Here, Rajabali turned the charge of "gaps" back on Barker. If invoking God as an explanation for a well-ordered, fine-tuned, conscious universe is a "gap," then declaring that there is no God—in spite of the same evidence—is likewise a gap-filling move. It is a metaphysical conclusion drawn not from an exhaustive understanding of reality, but from a commitment to naturalistic closure in the absence of total understanding.

Rajabali's point is that design in nature, the intelligibility of physical laws, and the emergence of moral consciousness are not unknowns—but known features of the universe. The theist is not appealing to ignorance, but to intelligible phenomena that cry out for sufficient explanation. His argument is therefore not: "We don't know, therefore God," but rather: "We do know—and God is the best explanation."

The Argument from Design: Not Plugging a Hole, But Tracing an Origin:

Barker repeatedly asserted that natural selection, geometry, and natural laws account for the appearance of design, and thus invoking God is unnecessary. He said:

> "There is design by Natural Selection... the design of how molecules combine... is design by the laws of nature."

But Rajabali's argument did not deny the operation of physical laws. Instead, he asked: Why do such laws exist in the first place? Why is the universe rationally ordered? Why do systems like evolution function in a framework that permits complexity, life, and consciousness?

Far from plugging gaps, Rajabali sought to explain the preconditions of intelligibility themselves. Laws of nature are not self-explanatory. Their precision, mathematical elegance, and ability to give rise to life require an ontological ground. As many philosophers of science have noted, the regularities of nature suggest not randomness but fine-tuned structure, which raises metaphysical questions beyond what physics alone can answer.[1]

The "God of the Gaps" accusation may have bite when applied to premature supernatural claims about weather, disease, or astronomical anomalies—areas once ascribed to deities but now better explained by science. But that is not the kind of argument Rajabali made. His reasoning was philosophical, not scientific, rooted in:

» The principle of sufficient reason

» The distinction between contingent and necessary being

» The intelligibility and order of the cosmos

» The presence of moral awareness and rational agency

These are not gaps in data, but deep structural features of reality that any worldview—naturalistic or theistic—must account for.

The Burden of Naturalism:

Ironically, it is Barker who seems to appeal to ignorance by refusing to address how naturalism explains these deeper realities. When asked by Rajabali how reason, value, and purpose emerge from a mindless universe, Barker deflected to evolutionary functions or human consensus—yet offered no account of how impersonal matter gives rise to meaning or moral objectivity.

---

[1] Much like trying to explain the software of a computer solely through its hardware, without reference to the programmer who wrote the code, reducing the intelligibility of the universe to natural laws without accounting for the source of those laws begs the very question of origin and intent that theism addresses. (Ed.)

This is why Rajabali said:

> "But then you turn quickly and say, if everything has a design, and the design has a designer, then the designer has a designer. Well, I told you earlier, and you apparently did not understand."

Rajabali was pointing out that Barker fails to distinguish between contingent causal chains and metaphysical necessity. God, as conceived in Islamic philosophy, is not just another being in the causal chain—He is the uncaused cause, the necessary being, without whom nothing contingent could exist. To ask "Who designed the designer?" is to fundamentally misunderstand the argument.

In conclusion, Dan Barker's invocation of the God of the Gaps critique oversimplifies—and ultimately misrepresents—the theistic arguments made by Hassanain Rajabali. The debate was not about appealing to ignorance but about competing explanations for the most profound features of reality: the existence of the universe, the order of nature, the presence of consciousness, and the grounding of morality.

Rajabali did not plug gaps—he offered a coherent metaphysical foundation. Barker, by contrast, insisted on the absence of evidence while himself declining to provide a fully developed alternative account. In that light, it is not the theist who is guilty of a "gap," but the naturalist—whose rejection of God leaves the deepest questions unanswered.

God: Beyond Frame of Reference

Hassanain Rajabali emphasizes the Islamic theological view that God (Allah) is not a being confined within the categories of time, space, matter, or relative definitions. He critiques Barker's arguments for consistently placing God within a "relative framework," which, according to Rajabali, is both philosophically and theologically inappropriate.

Rajabali states clearly:

> "God is the Absolute Creator. He has no frame of reference. Thus,

to put Him in a frame of reference implies that He is limited, and in reality, God is not limited"

This is a response to both the ontological and epistemological challenges posed by atheists, who ask questions like: "Where is God?", "What does He look like?", or "How can an unlimited being be a person?" Rajabali's rebuttal is that such questions are based on a misunderstanding: they apply created categories to the Creator.

He draws upon Qur'anic descriptions, such as:

Qul huwallāhu Aḥad, Allāhus-Ṣamad, meaning "Say: He is Allah, the One, Allah, the Self-sufficient" (Qur'an 112:1-2), to support the claim that God is indivisible, without dependency, and cannot be compartmentalized like created beings

He continues:

> "The relative world cannot exist without an Absolute Creator... Time is a creation of God. Matter is a creation of God. These are transient entities. Transient entities cannot come into existence by themselves"

From this theological framework, Rajabali explains that language about God is inherently limited. Humans, who are dependent on "frames of reference," are not equipped to speak of the Absolute Being in fully comprehensible or exhaustive terms. Therefore, even if God communicates attributes such as Merciful, Just, or Knowing, these are conveyed in a manner digestible by finite human understanding—not because God is compartmentalized, but because we are.

He reinforces this by stating:

> "The attributes are not separate entities of God... this infinite God is communicating to us due to our limitation. And our limitation should not imply therefore that we take our limitation and apply it on God"

Barker challenged the coherence of an absolute God by arguing that if God has no limits, then He cannot be a person. He stated:

> "To be a person means you have limits... But a being who has no limits... cannot be said, then, to be a person. Because there's no way to know what is not him."

In Barker's view, being a "person" necessitates some form of definition, contrast, or limitation. Without boundaries, the concept becomes meaningless. Therefore, defining God as an "infinite being" makes Him indistinguishable from "nothingness"—Barker sarcastically refers to God as an "infinite blob of nothingness." This rhetorical attack was designed to show that the theistic conception of God is too abstract to be meaningful

To this, Rajabali answers:

> "When we say that God is bound in time, how did He know tomorrow—tomorrow is not a substantive matter to question about God. God has no tomorrow. He knows... His knowledge is infinite in the absolute sense... and absolute cannot be defined, but we understand it indirectly"

Summary of Rajabali's Key Points:

a. God is Absolute –not confined by time, space, or matter. These are created entities.

b. Human Limitation –Our perception is inherently framed by relativity. Thus, our language and concepts fail to capture the essence of the Absolute.

c. Indirect Knowledge –The Islamic view supports indirect access to understanding God through His creation, attributes, and moral guidance, not through direct empirical means.

d. Rejection of Anthropomorphism –Trying to describe God in

human terms is, from his perspective, fundamentally flawed and amounts to "compartmentalization" of the divine.

e. Philosophical Consistency – Any attempt to define God using relative categories inevitably leads to contradiction or trivialization (e.g., calling God a "blob of nothingness").

f. Relevance to the Debate – His insistence on God's absoluteness is crucial in countering Barker's critiques, which rely heavily on testing God by empirical or logical constraints suited for the relative world.

By invoking God as an infinite, necessary Being, Rajabali emphasized the futility of attempting to empirically capture the transcendent. This is a bold move, as it effectively shifts the burden of the debate: rather than defending God as a hypothesis within the universe, Rajabali invites us to rethink what kind of explanation the universe itself demands.

Reframing the Debate:

This philosophical move challenges both atheists and theists to re-express the debate in more nuanced metaphysical terms. Instead of asking, "Is there a being somewhere in the universe who acts like a deity?"—the question becomes:

> "Is the universe intelligible without postulating a necessary, transcendent source of being, value, and order?"

Rajabali argues that the answer is no—and that calling this source "God" is not a matter of naming, but of ontological recognition.

Conclusion:

Rajabali's approach aligns closely with classical Islamic theology, particularly that of the rationalist *kalām* tradition and thinkers like Avicenna and Allamah Tabataba'i. His assertions are consistent throughout the debate, and his response to Barker's criticisms of an "unknowable, undefined god" is to clarify that it is not due to vagueness, but due to transcendence.

Thus, Rajabali did not avoid the issue of defining God—he redefined the very terms of engagement. In doing so, he shifted the conversation from trying to confine the Absolute within the limits of the finite, to recognizing that any such effort is metaphysically and epistemologically inappropriate.

The 'Married Bachelor' Analogy

Dan Barker introduced a provocative analogy in an effort to undermine the coherence of theism. He stated:

> "Suppose God is defined as a 'married bachelor.' Does He exist? You cannot ask 'Does He exist?', but you can just say 'He cannot exist.' A 'married bachelor' is discrepant. You can't have such a thing. And there are about a dozen different ways that God has been defined in the revealed religions that are mutually incompatible, definitions of God that cannot exist in the same being."

This rhetorical move is intended to frame the concept of God as logically incoherent, thereby suggesting that belief in such a being is not just false, but nonsensical. While the analogy is clever on the surface, a closer philosophical analysis reveals that Barker's argument is flawed both in its premises and application.

To begin with, Barker's observation is partially valid in a limited logical sense: If a concept is self-contradictory—such as a "married bachelor"—then it cannot exist in any possible world. This is a legitimate insight from formal logic. However, the key question is whether the classical theistic concept of God is truly self-contradictory.

Most revealed religions, particularly Islam, Christianity, and Judaism, define God using attributes such as:

Necessity (must exist)

Eternity (not bound by time)

Omniscience, Omnipotence, Omnibenevolence

Transcendence and Immanence

Unity (*tawḥīd* in Islam)

These attributes are complex and abstract, but they are not mutually exclusive or logically incompatible when understood in their proper philosophical and theological contexts. Throughout history, theologians like Mullā Ṣadrā have articulated coherent models that reconcile these attributes in rational systems. Islamic *kalām* traditions in particular have been vigilant in guarding the consistency of God's nature, maintaining that God's attributes do not imply multiplicity or contradiction within His essence.

Barker's further claim—that "there are about a dozen different ways God has been defined in the revealed religions that are mutually incompatible"—commits a category mistake. That various religious traditions define God differently does not mean each internal definition is contradictory. Instead, it means that not all of them can be simultaneously true—a very different claim. The existence of competing models does not invalidate all models, just as the presence of multiple cosmologies in history (e.g., geocentrism vs. heliocentrism) does not invalidate the existence of the cosmos.

Furthermore, Barker neglects the crucial distinction between contradiction and mystery. A contradiction violates the law of non-contradiction (e.g., A and not-A at the same time), whereas a mystery may simply refer to something not fully comprehensible within the bounds of human cognition—especially when dealing with metaphysical concepts like God, eternity, or necessary existence.

Indeed, Rajabali himself anticipated this category error in his argument. He emphasized that God, as the Absolute, transcends the relative framework of human understanding and empirical verification.

To attempt to "fit" God into empirical categories—subject to time, location, or form—is to engage in semantic and philosophical distortion. The apparent contradictions arise not from God's essence, but from attempts to force the Absolute into relative terms, much like trying to measure infinity with a ruler.

Finally, while Barker referenced evolution and empirical reasoning to ground his secular worldview, he failed to show how these tools can falsify or even meaningfully address transcendent claims. To claim that something like "God" is a contradiction demands rigorous analytic demonstration, not analogy or assertion.

In summary, Barker's "married bachelor" analogy, while rhetorically sharp, fails to accurately capture the intellectual coherence of classical theism. It misrepresents the nature of divine attributes, conflates religious diversity with logical incompatibility, and overlooks the long-standing philosophical traditions that have carefully articulated a unified, rational conception of God. Rather than exposing contradictions, Barker's analogy highlights the limitations of empirical and rhetorical reasoning when applied to metaphysical subjects that, by definition, transcend sensory categories.

Barker's "One Less God" Argument

Dan Barker's argument here unfolds in a rhetorical progression familiar in atheist discourse, particularly in popular debates. He uses the "one less god" analogy, defines atheism broadly, and concludes with a positive claim that the Abrahamic God—specifically Allah—does not exist. While rhetorically effective, the argument suffers from multiple philosophical oversights and an oversimplified representation of theistic belief.

1. The "One Less God" Analogy

> "The only difference between you and me is that I believe in one less god than you do."

This analogy is catchy but deeply misleading. The gods of the Greeks, Norsemen, and Mayans (e.g., Zeus, Thor, Quetzalcoatl) are finite, contingent, and anthropomorphic beings—essentially superhuman entities within the universe. In contrast, the Abrahamic concept of God (particularly in Islamic theology) is fundamentally different: a necessary, uncaused, timeless, transcendent being who grounds all existence.

By equating the rejection of polytheistic gods with the rejection of Allah, Barker commits a category mistake. The Islamic *shahāda* (*lā ilāha illā Allāh* = there is no god but Allah) is not denying contingent deities in the same category as Allah, but rather denying the divinity of anything that is not the Absolute. This is an ontological distinction, not just a numerical one.

Hassanain Rajabali responded to this logic elsewhere in the debate by emphasizing that God is the Necessary Being—not one god among many, but the ontological ground of all existence. He stated:

> "Whatever that answer you're going to give me has to be God... Supreme Power is what we are discussing. How you name it is based on your own perception."

This implies that names may vary, but the core metaphysical necessity remains. Thus, Barker's "one less god" trope doesn't land against a theistic worldview grounded in metaphysical necessity.

2. Defining Atheism and Making a Knowledge Claim

Barker distinguishes between:

» lower-case "a" atheism: the absence of belief

» upper-case "A" Atheism: the positive claim that specific gods do not exist

He then declares:

> "I am convinced and I claim to know that those gods—the Christian god, Allah—do not exist."

This is a bold epistemological stance. To claim to "know" that a being like Allah does not exist requires:

- » A full grasp of the concept being denied
- » A demonstration of internal contradiction or incompatibility with reality
- » Sufficient metaphysical grounds to rule out its existence

However, Barker does not directly engage with Islamic arguments that present God as a necessary, absolute, and non-contingent being, nor does he address Islamic philosophical theology (*kalām*) that argues for God's existence from contingency, design, or moral grounding. Instead, he frames his atheism based on a lack of empirical evidence, echoing:

"If there is a god, where is he or she or it?"

This question, while emotionally charged, ignores the theistic claim that God transcends sensory categories. Rajabali tackled this head-on when he explained that God, as Absolute, cannot be confined to empirical reference points:

> "The infinite power is a necessity... anything less than that is not sufficient."

This wasn't just rhetoric—it was a rejection of the attempt to treat God like a measurable object, which Barker implicitly does in his challenge.

3. The Appeal to Divine Hiddenness

Barker quotes Isaiah: "Truly you are a god who hides himself" (Isaiah

45:15) to support the claim that God's existence is not obvious.

This is a well-known philosophical objection—the argument from divine hiddenness—but again, it is insufficient to justify a claim of non-existence. Rajabali, though not explicitly addressing divine hiddenness in this debate, consistently emphasized that belief is about recognition, conscience, and seeking—not about coercive displays of power.

Moreover, the Islamic tradition posits that signs of God are embedded in creation (*āyāt*) for those who reflect. The Qur'an (41:53) states: "We shall show them Our signs in the horizons and in themselves until it becomes clear to them that it is the truth." This offers a very different epistemic framework from Barker's demand for overt proof.

In conclusion, Barker's challenge hinges on clever phrasing and familiar secular tropes, but it falters when brought into dialogue with the actual metaphysical and theological claims of Islam. His analogy between Zeus and Allah ignores the ontological chasm between mythological deities and the Necessary Being of classical theism. His epistemological claim to "know" Allah does not exist is unsupported by direct engagement with the arguments for His existence, especially as presented by Rajabali. And his appeal to divine hiddenness oversimplifies a deeply explored theological and philosophical issue.

Rajabali, for his part, responded with an ontological framework: God is not just "a being," but the basis of all being. That is a category unto itself—one that requires serious engagement, not just rhetorical dismissal.

Absence of Evidence or Evidence of Absence?

One of the most philosophically powerful moments in Hassanain Rajabali's opening statement during his debate with Dan Barker comes from a brief narration involving the Prophet Muhammad (peace be upon him). In it, a man approaches the Prophet and declares that he is an atheist because, in his view, the universe has always existed and therefore there is no need for a Creator. The Prophet asks the man whether he has seen God create the universe. The man replies no. The Prophet then turns the question around: "Have you seen that the universe always existed and will always exist?" Again, the man admits that he has not. The Prophet responds: "Then how come you have taken one side over the other? It is wiser for you to say, 'I don't know,' and I will subject myself to further scrutiny, than to take a stand and say 'There is no God,' because you have taken that stand and you have no evidence."

This short exchange crystallizes a central philosophical flaw in the hard atheist position—particularly one, like Dan Barker's, that confidently asserts: "There is no God," and then insists that there is "no evidence" for God's existence.

The Prophet's logic exposes not only the premature epistemic certainty of such a stance, but also the double standard often employed by those who reject God's existence while embracing competing metaphysical assumptions without sufficient warrant.

In making the claim that "there is no God," Barker is not merely suspending belief or expressing doubt—he is making a positive ontological assertion about reality. The Prophet's dialogue with the man who says the universe is eternal points to a subtle but critical problem: neither the eternal past nor the eternal future of the universe is observable or knowable through empirical means. To claim the universe "has always existed" is as speculative as claiming to have observed its divine creation. Yet, the man in the narration chose to believe in one view while rejecting the other, not because of evidence, but because of the absence of direct observation of God's creative act.

This is the very error the Prophet highlights: drawing a conclusion in favor of one ontological assumption over another in the absence of sufficient evidence for either, and doing so as if that absence counts as disproof of the alternative. It is, in modern terms, an appeal to ignorance—a fallacy that argues that something is false simply because it hasn't been proven true.

Dan Barker and the "No Evidence" Claim:

Dan Barker echoes this same epistemic misstep in the debate when he says:

> "Some people say that the absence of evidence is not the evidence of absence. But I disagree. If something is truly not existent, then the only evidence we can possibly have for its non-existence would be the absence of evidence for its existence. The absence of evidence is not proof, but it is certainly evidence. If god is obvious, and if god does exist, if there is evidence for it, then why are we having this debate?"

The implication here is that belief in God requires direct empirical evidence, and without it, belief is irrational. But Barker does not apply the same standard to the metaphysical alternatives he appears to accept—such as the self-sufficiency of the universe, the adequacy of naturalistic explanations, or the ontological status of reason and morality.

In the narration recounted by Rajabali, the Prophet challenges this kind of reasoning by shifting the burden back onto the atheist: "Have you seen that the universe always existed?" The question is not a mere rhetorical flourish—it is a challenge to intellectual honesty. If one is to suspend belief due to lack of evidence, then one must suspend belief on all metaphysical claims equally—including the idea that the universe has always existed without a cause.

The Prophet does not insist that the man accept God's existence blindly. Rather, he encourages him to admit uncertainty and then engage in further scrutiny. This is crucial. Theistic belief, especially in Islamic theology, is not founded merely on blind faith—it is rooted in rational inference, contemplation (*taʿaqqul*), and reflection on contingency, order, purpose, and moral consciousness.

The absence of direct empirical observation of God does not negate the availability of rational indicators (*āyāt*) that point toward a necessary, intelligent, and transcendent cause. These include:

The fine-tuning of the universe,

The existence of moral obligation,

The self-conscious rational mind,

The contingent nature of all physical reality.

All of these invite the rational mind to ask: "What explains these features of existence?" Theism offers an answer through the concept of a necessary being (*wājib al-wujūd*). Naturalism and atheism, by contrast, often retreat to brute fact or silence, offering no more than a negation—and often one made without sufficient philosophical grounding.

True Skepticism vs. Premature Denial:

The Prophet's advice to the man was not to believe uncritically, but to admit: "I don't know," and to pursue truth through investigation. This is the very essence of philosophical skepticism—a state of inquiry, not of denial. Barker, however, moves beyond skepticism and into dogmatic atheism, claiming to "know" that God does not exist, based on the supposed lack of evidence.

But as the Prophet's exchange demonstrates, lack of personal experience or direct observation does not constitute disproof—especially when the very nature of what is being discussed (God, eternity, necessity) lies beyond empirical reach. To insist on such evidence is to impose the wrong epistemological standard on a metaphysical question.

In conclusion the narration presented by Hassanain Rajabali stands as a timeless epistemological challenge: beliefs about the unseen, whether theism or naturalism, require intellectual humility. The claim that God does not exist is not the default rational position—it is a claim like any other, and it must be defended with arguments, not merely declared in the absence of physical observation.

Dan Barker's insistence on "no evidence" for God rests on a narrow and empiricist view of knowledge—one that even his own worldview cannot fully justify. The Prophet's response reminds us that true inquiry begins not with dogmatic denial, but with honest questioning, open investigation, and a willingness to say, "I don't know, but I will seek."

Characterization of the Qur'an

In his closing remarks, Dan Barker made a sweeping claim about the nature of the Qur'an, grouping it together with the Bible as what he called "books of war." He stated:

> "The Bible and the Qur'an are apparently your source of information about this god you worship. It didn't just come out of the air. Both books, if you read them—and I have really enjoyed reading some of the Qur'an, though I am not an expert in them—but if you get to the bottom, they both are really books of war. They are books 'versus them,' fighting. The god of those books is the God of War."

At first glance, this statement may seem to resonate with popular criticisms levied against religious texts in general, particularly when taken in isolation. However, upon closer scrutiny, Barker's assertion is both historically and hermeneutically problematic, especially with respect to the Qur'an.

1. Contextual Interpretation of Qur'anic Verses

One of the foundational principles of Qur'anic exegesis (*tafsīr*) is that verses must be interpreted within their historical and textual context. The Qur'an addresses a wide array of human situations—personal, ethical, legal, and socio-political—and many of its verses regarding warfare were revealed in specific historical circumstances, particularly in defense of the nascent Muslim community during times of persecution and military aggression.

For instance, when verses like "Fight in the way of Allah those who fight you but do not transgress. Indeed, Allah does not like transgressors" (Qur'an 2:190) are read selectively, they appear aggressive. But the full passage, when examined, lays down strict ethical limits on warfare—prohibiting aggression, urging restraint, and emphasizing peace when the enemy inclines toward peace (see Qur'an 8:61).

To call such a text a "book of war" is to strip it of its ethical depth, its emphasis on justice, and its call to spiritual and moral refinement. It is equivalent to calling the U.S. Constitution a "document of war" because it includes provisions about declaring war and commanding armies.

2. Defensive Warfare and Ethical Frameworks

The Qur'an never glorifies war as an ideal. Rather, it acknowledges that conflict is sometimes necessary, particularly to defend the rights of the oppressed, to resist persecution, and to protect religious freedom. Verses such as:

> "Permission [to fight] has been given to those who are being fought because they were wronged…" (Qur'an 22:39)

> "Had Allah not repelled some people by means of others, monasteries, churches, synagogues, and mosques—wherein the name of God is much mentioned—would have been demolished." (Qur'an 22:40)

…reveal a vision of warfare that is not rooted in conquest or fanaticism, but in preserving human dignity, pluralism, and freedom of conscience.

3. Misapplication of "God of War"

To characterize the God of the Qur'an as a "God of War" is to flatten a richly nuanced theological portrayal into a one-dimensional caricature. The Qur'an opens with "In the Name of Allah, the All-Beneficent, the All-Merciful"—attributes that occur over 100 times throughout the text. It presents God as the source of life, mercy, guidance, justice, and forgiveness. Even when punishment or justice is invoked, it is tied to moral accountability and cosmic order, not divine bloodlust.

Indeed, the Qur'anic narrative prioritizes:

Mercy over punishment (Qur'an 6:12)

Forgiveness over retaliation (Qur'an 41:34)

Peace over conflict (Qur'an 8:61)

The Prophet Muhammad's own conduct during war—highlighted by rules that forbade harming civilians, women, children, and destroying nature—reflects the Qur'an's ethical framework, not the image of a militaristic deity.

4. A Selective Reading by Barker

Barker admits, "I am not an expert," and this humility is appreciated. However, it also underscores a critical point: a fair and rigorous assessment of any religious scripture requires engagement with its commentarial tradition, linguistic nuances, and historical backdrop. Without these tools, one risks falling into superficial generalizations that obscure far more than they reveal.

In a debate of such philosophical depth, it is unfortunate that Barker resorted to a reading of the Qur'an that mirrors polemical interpretations often divorced from serious scholarship.

In conclusion, the Qur'an is not a "book of war." It is a book of guidance, addressing the realities of human life, including conflict, but always through a lens of divine mercy, ethical accountability, and justice. To reduce it to a militaristic manifesto is to misread its message and to ignore its overarching spiritual and moral aims.

Dan Barker's claim may serve rhetorical effect, but it lacks the scholarly nuance and interpretive fairness expected in meaningful dialogue. Rather than drawing lines of hostility based on misunderstood verses, genuine inquiry must begin with context, curiosity, and care—virtues the Qur'an itself enjoins upon all who seek to understand.

Critique Of Richard Carrier's Review[1]

Introduction

Richard Carrier's review of the "Does God Not Exist?" debate between Hassanain Rajabali and Dan Barker offers a sharp and articulate atheist perspective, rich in rhetorical skill and philosophical positioning. His analysis has been circulated in secular circles and is often cited as a model for post-debate reflection. However, while the review is intellectually engaging, it contains several significant misreadings of both the structure and substance of Rajabali's arguments.

This critique does not aim to undermine Carrier's credibility as a scholar, but to correct mischaracterizations, clarify key theological distinctions, and evaluate the philosophical depth of both debaters more evenly. Most importantly, it seeks to offer readers a more balanced understanding of what was actually argued in the debate, especially where Carrier's framing oversimplifies or prematurely dismisses complex metaphysical positions.

As public discourse on faith and reason grows increasingly polarized, engaging critically—and fairly—with prominent reviews like Carrier's is essential to preserving intellectual honesty, philosophical rigor, and mutual understanding across worldviews.

This critique is divided into five sections:[2]

---

[1] The full text of Richard Carrier's review can be found using this web address: infidels.org/library/modern/review-of-the-barker-rajabali-debate/#Team

[2] This division is based on Carrier's review in the order he presented. (Ed.)

- » Argument from the Universe

- » Argument from Absolute Morality

- » The "Trial" Defense versus the Argument from Evil

- » Shoring up Agnosticism

- » Pitching Balls for the Home Team

Argument From Universe

Richard Carrier introduces what he dubs the "Argument from the Universe"—a term he uses to characterize the overarching structure of Hassanain Rajabali's case for theism. Carrier argues that Rajabali's position is a "conflation" of three traditionally distinct arguments: the Ontological, Cosmological, and Design arguments. He further suggests that Rajabali seemed "unaware of these distinctions," resulting in an argument that was "muddled and hard to pin down." Carrier labels the overall approach "Evidential Presuppositionalism," a phrase meant to distinguish it from more familiar (and, in his view, equally flawed) forms of Christian presuppositional apologetics.

Carrier's framing is rhetorically effective, yet philosophically and analytically problematic. His interpretation of Rajabali's approach is based on a reductionist reading of the debate, one that misrepresents the structure of Rajabali's reasoning and overlooks both the thematic coherence and the metaphysical precision of his argumentation.

Carrier's charge that Rajabali "conflated" three separate arguments—Ontological, Cosmological, and Design—fails to appreciate the integrated method Rajabali employed. It is true that Rajabali did not explicitly label or formally separate these classical arguments, but his strategy was deliberately cumulative rather than confused.

Throughout the debate, Rajabali weaves together cosmological reflection (e.g., the dependency of the universe), teleological insights (e.g., the order and intelligibility of nature), and metaphysical reasoning (e.g., the necessity of a non-contingent ground). This method is not philosophically incoherent; it reflects a style of reasoning that is common among classical theists, including thinkers like Mulla Ṣadrā in Islamic philosophy and Thomas Aquinas in Christian scholasticism.

Moreover, Rajabali repeatedly stated that the universe—by virtue of being relative and contingent—cannot account for its own existence:

> "How does a relative universe come into existence by itself? Whatever that answer is, it has to be God… an infinite power is a necessity; anything less than that is not sufficient."

Such statements reflect a metaphysical argument from contingency, not a mere blending of arguments due to conceptual confusion. Far from being "muddled," Rajabali's approach aimed to show that the entire structure of reality—its existence, order, and intelligibility—points toward a necessary, non-contingent source.

Carrier's term "Evidential Presuppositionalism" is rhetorically clever but ultimately misleading. It attempts to synthesize two schools of apologetics—presuppositionalism (which often starts with the necessity of God for the intelligibility of reason) and evidentialism (which appeals to observable facts). Carrier claims that Rajabali's method is "presuppositionalist" because it insists that "you can never have a universe like the one we observe without a god."

However, Rajabali does not merely assert this as an unargued presupposition. He presents arguments from contingency and order to support the view that a necessary being is the best explanation for the universe's existence. The philosophical tradition behind this reasoning is not presuppositionalist in the Van Tilian or Bahnsenian sense; it is a posteriori and metaphysically grounded.

By calling it presuppositionalism, Carrier implies circularity or dogmatic insulation from critique. But Rajabali welcomed rational inquiry and engaged the metaphysical implications of cosmology, moral realism, and human consciousness. Carrier's label thus misrepresents the openness and intellectual structure of Rajabali's position.

Carrier describes the Ontological, Cosmological, and Design arguments as "old arguments that have long been refuted." This is a sweeping generalization that ignores the ongoing, serious defense of these arguments in contemporary philosophy of religion. Moreover, even if one finds these arguments unconvincing, it does not follow that they are muddled or obsolete. They remain central to philosophical discourse precisely because they raise enduring questions about the nature of existence, causality, and design.

Carrier's framing of Rajabali's core argument as a "conflated pea soup" does more to serve rhetorical strategy than philosophical clarity. Rajabali's position—though not labeled according to academic taxonomy—was internally coherent, thematically unified, and rooted in a metaphysical tradition that aims to explain the necessary preconditions for existence, order, and intelligibility.

What Carrier calls "Evidential Presuppositionalism" is better understood as a cumulative metaphysical case for a necessary being. Rajabali's reasoning, far from being confused, reflects a systematic worldview shaped by both Islamic theology and classical philosophical inquiry.

A. The Ontological Argument:

Richard Carrier suggests that one of the three classic theistic arguments implicitly embedded in Hassanain Rajabali's macro-argument was the Ontological Argument—though not formally presented as such.

Carrier observes that Rajabali "never makes anything like a formal defense of this argument," but "clearly implies it at several points in the debate, like when he says that nothing can come from nothing, therefore something must necessarily exist that brought everything about, and that is God." In other words, Rajabali seems to be asserting that since nothing can arise from nothing, there must be a necessary being—and that being is God.

However, Carrier contends that this claim conflates ontological necessity with metaphysical assumption. He praises Dan Barker for responding by suggesting that the universe itself—or some non-conscious fundamental reality—could be the necessary being, but criticizes Barker for not elaborating further. According to Carrier, naturalistic alternatives like the "underlying nature of the universe," or even a dimensionless primordial state, could serve as a metaphysical ground without invoking God.

Carrier adds that under certain interpretations of determinism, such as B-Theory (the view that all events in time are equally real), there is "no such thing as a contingent being—all beings are necessary—making the entire universe its own necessary being."

This objection challenges Rajabali's inference from "necessary existence" to "personal God." But as the debate transcript shows, Rajabali's intention was less about formal ontological reasoning and more about pointing out the absurdity of self-creation or emergence from nothing, which he claimed violates both rational intuition and causality.

While Rajabali may not have framed this point as the traditional Anselmian Ontological Argument,[1] his appeal to necessary being through causality and dependency aligns closely with Islamic theological reasoning, particularly the view that existence itself points to a

---

1 The Anselmian Ontological Argument is a classical formulation by St. Anselm of Canterbury (1033–1109), which asserts that God, being "that than which nothing greater can be conceived," must exist in reality because existence is a necessary component of maximal greatness. If God exists only in the mind, then a greater being—one that exists both in the mind and in reality—could be conceived, leading to a contradiction. This a priori argument seeks to prove God's existence purely through logical reasoning, without recourse to empirical evidence. (Ed.)

reality that is not dependent, divisible, or contingent—and that only such a reality could account for the universe.

Thus, Carrier's critique is instructive, but possibly underestimates the theological framework Rajabali was drawing from—one that does not strictly rely on the Ontological Argument in its Western formulation, but rather combines ontological and cosmological intuitions into a broader metaphysical worldview.[1]

B. The Cosmological Argument:

A focal point of Carrier's review was Rajabali's use of the Cosmological Argument, which he identified as one of several conflated arguments under Rajabali's broader "Argument from the Universe." While Carrier's assessment is more philosophically nuanced than some of his earlier critiques, it still suffers from selective reading and underappreciates the coherence of Rajabali's metaphysical reasoning. Meanwhile, Carrier rightly critiques Barker's counter-response for lacking sufficient elaboration.

The Cosmological Argument, in its classical form, argues from contingency to necessity or from temporal causation to a First Cause. While it takes different forms—Kalam, Thomistic, Leibnizian—all share a central intuition: that contingent beings require a cause, and the chain of contingent causes cannot regress infinitely.[2] Therefore,

---

[1] A broader metaphysical worldview refers to a comprehensive philosophical outlook that integrates concepts such as existence, causality, purpose, necessity, and contingency into a unified understanding of reality. In the context of Islamic theism, this worldview does not isolate arguments (e.g., ontological, cosmological, teleological) into strict categories but instead presents a holistic metaphysical framework in which the existence of God is seen as the necessary foundation for all contingent reality and intelligibility. (Auth.)

[2] Rajabali illustrates this principle in his second debate with Barker using the

a necessary, uncaused cause must exist, which is identified as God.

In the debate, Rajabali repeatedly emphasized themes central to this tradition:

» Nothing comes from nothing.
» There must be a necessary cause behind this universe.
» The universe had a beginning and cannot bring itself into existence.

He also referenced the Big Bang, not to make a scientific argument per se, but to support the premise that the universe had a beginning—a position consistent with most current cosmological models. In doing so, Rajabali implicitly followed the logic of the Kalam Cosmological Argument:

» Whatever begins to exist has a cause.
» The universe began to exist.
» Therefore, the universe has a cause.

Carrier accurately identifies that Rajabali's argument depends on causation and empirical data, rather than on conceptual definitions (as in the Ontological Argument). However, the suggestion that Rajabali conflated arguments or presented them in a confused manner is unfounded. While Rajabali did not demarcate philosophical categories formally, his reasoning was both intelligible and consistent.

The Charge of an "Unelaborated" Argument: Partially Fair, but

---

analogy of a group of soldiers waiting to fire: "Imagine a battlefield where each soldier refuses to shoot until the soldier next to him shoots first. If no one takes the first shot, the war never begins." The point is that an infinite regress of dependent actions (or causes) would result in no effect at all. Therefore, for the universe—or any sequence of contingent events—to exist, there must be an initiating cause that is itself uncaused. This aligns with the classical intuition behind the Cosmological Argument: that a First Cause or Necessary Being must exist to ground all contingent reality. (Auth.)

Incomplete

Carrier critiques Rajabali's use of cosmology as "fairly unelaborated," suggesting he failed to delve into contemporary physics or alternative cosmological theories. This is partially true: Rajabali did not address multiverse theory, quantum gravity models, or other theorem counterpoints.

However, Rajabali's goal was metaphysical, not scientific. His aim was to interpret the existence and origin of the universe through the lens of rational metaphysics. By invoking the beginning of the universe and its contingent nature, he laid the groundwork for arguing that the universe cannot be the explanation of its own existence.

In this sense, Rajabali's approach was philosophically sufficient, even if it lacked scientific elaboration. It is not the role of a theist in such debates to exhaust the physics literature but to show that the metaphysical implication of a beginning is the necessity of a cause.

Carrier rightly observes that Dan Barker made some attempt to challenge the Cosmological Argument but ultimately did not develop his position adequately. Barker proposed that:

» The universe, or some part of it, might be eternal or necessary.
» The laws of physics might be self-sufficient or uncaused.
» Time and causation may break down at the Big Bang, rendering causal reasoning irrelevant.

These are plausible suggestions within the broader landscape of naturalistic metaphysics, and had they been fleshed out, they could have presented a meaningful counter to Rajabali's theism.

However, Barker did not engage with:

» The Principle of Sufficient Reason, which demands an explanation for why anything exists at all.

- » The philosophical problems with brute fact metaphysics, where things simply exist without explanation.

- » The distinction between abstract necessity (e.g., mathematics) and efficient causality (what brings about existence).

- » The challenge of grounding intentionality, rationality, and morality in an impersonal or mechanistic source.

As such, Barker's rebuttal remained assertive rather than demonstrative. He posed an alternative (a necessary universe) but did not justify it as a superior explanation to theism.

Perhaps the most incisive point Carrier raises is that Barker's counter-argument simultaneously invoked the universe as its own necessary being and its own cause—without distinguishing between these concepts.

In classical theism:

- » A necessary being is one whose existence is non-contingent and self-explanatory.

- » A cause is that which brings something into existence.

To say that the universe is its own cause introduces a logical contradiction: it must exist before it exists to bring itself into being. To say that it is a necessary being demands a defense of why its properties (contingency, change, entropy) can be squared with metaphysical necessity.

Rajabali, drawing from Islamic metaphysics, correctly insisted that nothing contingent can explain itself. If the universe exhibits change, complexity, and dependency, it cannot be necessary in the metaphysical sense. A genuine necessary being must be changeless, eternal, simple, and non-dependent—attributes traditionally ascribed to God.

By failing to distinguish these categories, Barker's position appeared philosophically shallow, despite his confidence.

In conclusion, the Cosmological Argument, as presented by Rajabali in the debate, was consistent, coherent, and grounded in classical metaphysics. While he did not formally distinguish it from other theistic proofs, his appeal to causation, contingency, and cosmic origins followed a recognizable philosophical tradition.

Carrier's assessment that Barker failed to adequately counter this argument is accurate. Barker offered naturalistic possibilities but did not provide a positive explanatory account that rivaled the theistic one. Moreover, by conflating metaphysical necessity with causal sufficiency, he blurred categories that classical metaphysics insists must remain distinct.

Ultimately, Rajabali's use of the Cosmological Argument was a central pillar of his case. While not exhaustively defended in terms of modern science, it was unrefuted in the debate, and Carrier's critique—though thoughtful—misrepresents it as confused or underdeveloped. On the contrary, Rajabali's argument retained philosophical integrity and rhetorical force, standing as one of the strongest elements of his defense.

C. The Argument to Design:

Another key argument employed by Rajabali was the Argument from Design—a theistic inference drawn from the order, precision, and intelligibility of the natural world. Richard Carrier argued that this was the third of three "conflated" arguments (along with cosmological and ontological reasoning) which, in his view, were not clearly distinguished by Rajabali. According to him, Rajabali relied on the Design Argument "to a far greater extent than the other two," using examples from biology and cosmology, while simultaneously accepting evolution—leading Carrier to accuse him of a "somewhat self-contradictory" position. Barker, Carrier claimed, successfully rebutted the biological elements of this argument but failed to engage with its cosmological (fine-tuning) dimensions.

While Carrier's observations regarding the emphasis Rajabali placed on design and the incompleteness of Barker's rebuttal are largely accurate, the claim of contradiction in Rajabali's position is philosophically unsound.

I. The Structure of Rajabali's Design Argument

The Argument from Design, also known as the Teleological Argument, is one of the oldest and most intuitively compelling arguments for the existence of God. It asserts that the complexity, order, and purpose found in nature are best explained by an intelligent designer. Rajabali's version of this argument, as reflected in the debate transcript, took two interlinked forms:

Biological Design: Rajabali pointed to the intricacy and coordination found in the human body, the interdependence of natural systems, and the emergence of consciousness and morality as indicative of purpose beyond mere material processes.

Cosmic Design (Fine-Tuning Argument): He also referenced the precise values of physical constants, the laws of physics, and the structure of the cosmos as evidence of a universe fine-tuned for life, which he argued cannot be plausibly attributed to chance or necessity alone.

Paraphrasing, he stated:

> "Evolution is a reality. But the very system that enables evolution, and the intelligence embedded within it, is what points to a Designer."[1]

---

[1] This is a fair summary of several statements he made during the debate such as "Natural selection is an entity that is part of the great design. You seem to have taken this thing (theory), and the pin hole vision of how an engine in the car does combustion and said 'that's it, we don't need to worry about the car itself, it is the combustion within the system that takes place, and that's sufficient for us.' Well, then that in itself is an incredible design."

This encapsulates his central thesis: that evolution does not eliminate design, but rather presupposes an intelligible, life-permitting order within which it operates. Far from being a contradiction, this view aligns with a long tradition of theistic evolution that sees natural processes as instruments of divine will, rather than rivals to it.[1]

II. Carrier's Claim of Contradiction: A Misunderstanding

Richard Carrier claims that Rajabali's acceptance of evolution[2] undermines his use of design-based reasoning. He writes:

> "His position here was somewhat self-contradictory, in that he openly accepted evolution as a natural phenomenon yet kept employing examples of its products as evidence of God's work. Barker rightly rebutted this by discussing the natural basis of evolution."

This accusation reflects a common misunderstanding of the philosophical compatibility between theistic belief and evolutionary science. In modern philosophy of religion and theology, many theists—including prominent thinkers from both Islamic and Christian traditions—affirm evolution as the mechanism through which life develops while maintaining that the underlying framework of the universe is designed or sustained by divine intelligence.

Rajabali's argument does not rest on rejecting evolution. On the

---

[1] Basically, Rajabali criticizes atheists for focusing only on natural mechanisms while refusing to address the system that makes those mechanisms possible. (Ed.)

[2] While Rajabali does not use the exact phrasing "Yes, I accept evolution," he clearly affirms the mechanism and its natural place within a broader system, which he attributes to divine design. He challenges atheists not on the mechanics of evolution but on their inability (from his perspective) to account for the framework that makes evolution intelligible or even possible. (Ed.)

contrary, he repeatedly affirmed that evolutionary processes are real. His point was that evolution itself—while explaining how species diversify—presupposes a universe finely tuned for such processes to occur. His design argument centered not on the direct intervention of God in each mutation or adaptation, but on the broader metaphysical question of why the universe permits evolution at all.

He pointed to three central features that require explanation:

» The ordered and intelligible structure of the universe

» The precision of physical laws that permit life and evolutionary development

» The emergence of conscious, moral, and rational beings

From this perspective, evolution operates within a created system—a system whose depth, intelligibility, and life-permitting properties suggest intentionality and purpose.

Carrier's claim of contradiction arises only if one assumes that belief in God necessarily entails rejection of natural processes like evolution. Rajabali's view, however, aligns with a non-interventionist or providential model of divine action: God creates a world embedded with potentialities, laws, and capacities that naturally give rise to complex life without requiring constant supernatural intervention.

In this light, Carrier's criticism fails to account for the philosophical nuance of Rajabali's position. Rather than being contradictory, it represents a coherent synthesis of scientific acceptance and theological interpretation—one that is increasingly common among contemporary theists.

III. Barker's Rebuttal: Effective on Biology, Silent on Cosmology

Barker responded to Rajabali's biological examples by emphasizing the natural basis of evolution and its ability to explain complexity without invoking design. He highlighted:

» Natural selection as a blind but effective mechanism.

» The existence of flawed or vestigial organs as counterexamples to perfect design.

» The success of evolutionary biology in predicting and explaining biodiversity.

These points are well-established in the scientific literature and were presented clearly in the debate. On the biological side of the argument, Barker's response was philosophically and empirically grounded.

However, Barker did not engage with the deeper cosmological dimension of Rajabali's Design Argument. Rajabali stated:

> "The constants that govern this universe are not arbitrary. They are finely set to allow life, and that points to intelligence."

This is a form of the Fine-Tuning Argument, which observes that the physical constants of the universe (e.g., the gravitational constant, the strong nuclear force, the mass of subatomic particles) lie within extraordinarily narrow ranges that allow for the emergence of life. Many philosophers and scientists, including Roger Penrose, Paul Davies, and Robin Collins, have argued that this fine-tuning demands explanation.

Barker never addressed:

» The possibility of cosmic design as a metaphysical explanation.

» The anthropic principle, multiverse theory, or necessity hypotheses as naturalistic alternatives.

» The distinction between designed systems and brute-fact explanations.

As such, the core of Rajabali's Design Argument—cosmic order—was left untouched in the debate. Barker focused on evolutionary biology, which Rajabali had already accepted, but did not challenge the metaphysical implications of a life-permitting universe.

IV. Philosophical Coherence of Rajabali's Position

Rajabali's argument, in its full structure, can be summarized as follows:

» Evolution is real, but presupposes a rational universe.

» The physical laws and constants that permit evolution are finely tuned.

» Such fine-tuning is best explained by intentional design.

» Therefore, the universe is the product of divine intelligence.

This framework avoids the "God of the gaps" fallacy because it does not insert God to explain what science hasn't yet figured out, but argues that the very possibility of science, order, and evolution presupposes a deeper rational ground—what classical theism identifies as God.

This position is neither scientifically regressive nor philosophically confused. Rather, it echoes centuries of metaphysical reflection that sees order, intelligibility, and finality in nature as pointing toward a non-material, intelligent source.

In conclusion, Hassanain Rajabali's use of the Design Argument in the debate was thoughtful, integrated, and consistent with theistic commitments that affirm evolution while attributing deeper order and purpose to the universe. While Dan Barker addressed the evolutionary dimension effectively, he did not engage with the cosmic architecture and fine-tuning dimensions of Rajabali's case.

As a result, a significant portion of the Design Argument remained unanswered, leaving Rajabali's claim—that the order of the universe reflects intelligence—as one of the stronger elements of his defense in the debate.

D. Imperfection, Necessity, and the Limits of Naturalism:

In the debate, questions of cosmic design, moral imperfection, and metaphysical necessity formed a substantial part of the theistic case presented by Hassanain Rajabali. Richard Carrier reflected on these elements, arguing that Rajabali contradicted himself in rejecting imperfection, failed to formally present a necessity argument, and relied on an unearned cumulative impression that atheists had no meaningful answers to the big questions. He stated:

"One argument that Barker used but didn't have time to capitalize on is that there is imperfection in creation, and that does not seem likely on the hypothesis that God created it. Rajabali rebutted this by saying that there were no imperfections in creation: it is only the imperfections in us that cause us to see the world incorrectly. It never dawned on him that this was self-refuting."

While this review captures several real dynamics in the debate, its conclusions rest on several misreadings and philosophical oversights that require clarification.

Imperfection and the Self-Refutation Fallacy:

Dan Barker briefly appealed to the problem of imperfection in creation, suggesting that if God is perfect, His creation should not contain flaws, evils, or inefficiencies. This is a subset of the classical Problem of Evil, but framed in functional rather than purely moral terms.

Rajabali's rebuttal was rooted in a teleological worldview: he did not deny the existence of death, suffering, or entropy. Rather, he argued that what we perceive as imperfections may be misunderstood, especially when viewed outside the full context of divine wisdom, eschatology, and moral trial. He positioned imperfection as an epistemic issue—what seems flawed from a limited human perspective may actually serve a higher good or reveal deeper purpose.

Carrier's counter—that if human beings are flawed, then creation must be flawed, and thus God's perfection is undermined—commits a category error. In theistic theology, human beings are created with limited faculties, free will, and susceptibility to error as part of their spiritual testing ground. This does not logically imply a flaw in divine action, but reflects a necessary condition for moral growth and genuine responsibility. Far from being self-refuting, Rajabali's answer is a philosophically consistent theodicy.

Necessity Without Syllogism: A Stylistic, Not Substantive, Gap

Carrier notes that Rajabali failed to present a formal syllogism for the claim that God is a necessary being. This is true. Rajabali's rhetorical strategy was philosophical and metaphysical, drawing on themes of:

Contingency (things that could not have existed), Causality (things that began to exist must have a cause), And intelligibility (order and consciousness suggest purpose).

While these were not framed as a tight deductive syllogism, they nonetheless pointed to a metaphysical necessity, not merely to a probabilistic conclusion. Rajabali's references to God as the "necessary source" and his insistence that "nothing comes from nothing" were clear attempts to ground theistic belief in metaphysical logic, even if informally presented.

Naturalism's Explanatory Silence on Cosmic Order:

Perhaps the most important insight Carrier offers is that, while atheists like Barker can explain biological evolution, they did not explain why the universe itself is structured in such a way as to allow evolution at all. Rajabali's argument was not simply about design in the outcome, but about the framework of reality itself:

Why are the laws of physics so orderly and mathematically intelligible?

Why do constants fall within narrow life-permitting ranges?

Why is the universe intelligible to minds like ours?

To these questions, Barker offered no sustained answers. He focused on empirical science, but remained silent on the metaphysical question of being: Why is there something rather than nothing?

In contrast, Rajabali's theism presented a holistic view where God is both the metaphysical ground of being and the teleological source of intelligible order.

Conclusion: Rhetorical Clarity vs. Metaphysical Coherence

Richard Carrier is correct to say that Barker's best arguments were underused and that Rajabali held rhetorical ground due to the structure and confidence of his presentation. However, the suggestion that Rajabali's case was philosophically weak, self-refuting, or merely probabilistic does not hold upon scrutiny.

Rajabali's view of imperfection aligns with standard theistic theodicies and was not contradictory.

His case for God as necessary being was implicit, though not syllogistically framed.

Most significantly, Barker left the central metaphysical questions unaddressed, allowing Rajabali's view to stand unrefuted.

In sum, Carrier's reflections are valuable but require correction on key points. Rajabali's argument was neither inconsistent nor superficial. If anything, it succeeded in exposing the philosophical limitations of a purely naturalistic framework, which, while strong in evolutionary biology, remains quiet on the foundations of existence itself.

Argument From Absolute Morality

In debates about the existence of God, the question of morality often emerges as one of the most emotionally and philosophically charged topics. In the exchange between Dan Barker and Hassanain Rajabali, this issue surfaced as a key focal point—one that elicited clear audience engagement and led to rhetorical victories for the theist. Richard Carrier identified Rajabali's "Argument from Absolute Morality" as his second most important line of reasoning, but dismissed it as fallacious, emotionally manipulative, and intellectually shallow. He writes:

"His [Rajabali's] argument, made repeatedly (so often in fact it clearly was his second most important argument), was that atheism entailed moral relativism, moral relativism is repugnant to us, therefore atheism is false. That is simply an egregious fallacy. Nevertheless, as always, it was rhetorically very effective and brought ample agreement from the crowd."

Upon closer inspection, however, this judgment requires revision.

Rajabali's argument was grounded not in emotional appeal or wishful thinking but in moral ontology and ethical standards. He repeatedly challenged Barker to explain not just how atheists can be moral, but why they ought to be—and why any moral claims should be binding or universal in a godless universe. He argued that in the absence of divine accountability, moral obligations become preferences, and moral relativism prevails. This argument is not new, but it is philosophically serious and has been taken seriously by both theistic and atheistic moral philosophers alike.

Carrier's dismissal of this argument as "fallacious" overlooks this rich tradition. Rajabali never claimed that the undesirability of moral relativism proves God exists. Rather, he claimed that atheism lacks the resources to ground moral objectivity, and that belief in God provides a more plausible explanatory framework. This is a version of what philosophers call an inference to the best explanation, not an emotional fallacy.

Meanwhile, Barker's ethical system—rooted in harm reduction and empathy—was articulated with clarity and sincerity. He spoke of moral progress, human wellbeing, and his own lived experience. However, as Carrier correctly notes, Barker never made a case for why his moral principles should be binding on others, or why they rise above cultural consensus or subjective preference. He never engaged with the theistic concern about ethical expectations, nor did he confront the charge that without an ultimate standard or enforcer, ethics become situational and negotiable.

This gap in Barker's response allowed Rajabali to press the advantage. Whether or not one agrees with theistic morality, it offers a clear framework: God is the source of objective moral truth; humans are accountable to Him; and moral law is grounded in divine nature. In contrast, Barker's humanist model—though appealing to reason and compassion—did not explain why those values should matter universally. The question "Why is it wrong to harm another person?" demands more than "Because we don't like it."

The discussion also briefly touched on the doctrine of hell, with Barker accusing theistic morality of being fear-based. This is a valid challenge to motivational purity, but not to moral ontology. Rajabali could have responded (though he did not explicitly) that the ultimate motive for goodness in theism is not fear, but love of God and alignment with divine will—a point well-established in Islamic spiritual literature. Nonetheless, the detour into the morality of hell distracted from the central debate about whether atheism can ground objective ethics.

In the end, the moral argument—flawed or not—was rhetorically powerful. The audience, as Carrier noted, was clearly moved by the question of whether atheists are morally trustworthy. This is a perception issue that atheist debaters must anticipate and address more robustly. Barker's moral consistency and evident kindness helped defuse some stereotypes, but he did not equip the audience with a philosophically compelling alternative to the theistic moral framework.

Thus, while Carrier is right to say that atheists must do better at defending moral foundations, his dismissal of Rajabali's argument as irrational is itself a misreading. Rajabali's critique of moral relativism was a legitimate philosophical challenge—and it went largely unanswered.

Trial Defense And Argument From Evil

Richard Carrier's comment on Hassanain Rajabali's defense against the Argument from Evil raises several interesting critiques that merit detailed evaluation. To assess the accuracy and fairness of the critique, it is essential to examine Rajabali's response to the problem of evil within the actual transcript of the debate, especially as it relates to suffering, divine justice, and the existence of evil in a divinely created world.

Rajabali's "Trial Defense": The Core of the Rebuttal

Rajabali did indeed advance what Carrier aptly calls the "Trial Defense." He articulated that evil is not an absolute but a relative entity necessary for the moral and spiritual development of human beings. The argument is rooted in Islamic theology, which views life as a divinely orchestrated test (*ibtilā'*), where moral decisions are meaningful only within a world that includes both good and evil.

He stated: "So from the Islamic perspective, it is a relativistic position, and evil is a trial... If the wrong did not exist, would we be able to debate? No! ... Good cannot be understood without that which is not good and is existing simultaneously".

Rajabali likened this to an exam, arguing that just as a teacher includes incorrect multiple-choice options to assess the student's knowledge, evil offers a frame of reference for appreciating and choosing good. He even went further to challenge the notion of a utopia where pain is nonexistent, calling such a concept "a preposterous mentality," using the example of invincible children to highlight the absurdity of such a hypothetical world.

Carrier's critique is twofold:

Logical Problem: If God is all-knowing, then He does not need to test us to discern who is righteous. Hence, the whole "trial" is unnecessary from God's perspective and merely subjects humans to needless suffering.

Moral Problem: The idea that God would allow children to suffer as part of a trial for others is seen as morally grotesque. Carrier argues that since we are part of creation, our imperfections reflect imperfections in creation itself, thereby undermining Rajabali's claim that creation is perfect.

These criticisms have merit, particularly from a naturalistic or humanistic standpoint. However, they also rely on certain assumptions that are not shared within Rajabali's theological framework. From an Islamic metaphysical view, divine foreknowledge does not negate human agency or the need for trials. The purpose of the test is not for God to learn anything new but for humans to realize and exercise their moral capacity. Rajabali made this clear:

"This trial is not for God to know, it is for man to know… the exam is not for the teacher to know what the student will do".

The "God Knows Best" Response:

Carrier further critiques Rajabali for invoking the "God knows best" defense, stating that such an argument is unfalsifiable and thus epistemologically invalid. Rajabali does imply that what appears as "gratuitous evil" may, in fact, have wisdom beyond human comprehension. He said:

"If one wants to say that evil should not exist, then earth should not exist… Rather we are in a system where we understand that evil is there".

This argument aligns with classical Islamic theology, which posits that God's knowledge is absolute and that human understanding is inherently limited. While this renders the claim unfalsifiable, it is consistent within the religious worldview. To an external critic, however, this may appear as a form of dogmatic evasion.

Barker's Response: Missed Opportunities

Carrier is justified in saying that Dan Barker did not thoroughly address Rajabali's "Trial Defense." Barker's rebuttal focused more on moral outrage and rhetorical critique rather than analytic dismantling. For instance, he said:

"So, if your god is all good, he is on trial… He apparently cares more about the free will of Christian, Jewish and Islamic terrorists, than he does about the precious human lives, which could have been saved".

While emotionally powerful, this response does not directly address Rajabali's nuanced theological defense rooted in divine wisdom and the moral necessity of suffering. A more pointed critique could have involved demonstrating how unnecessary suffering (e.g., from natural disasters or genetic diseases) fails even the internal logic of divine testing.

Richard Carrier's Final Comment: "Lack of Compassion"?

Carrier accuses Rajabali of a lack of "compassion and imagination," interpreting his rejection of invincible children as a mocking dismissal of suffering. He says in his review:

"Now for a personal observation. Rajabali's defense of God against the charge of cruelty is reprehensible and betrays a startling lack of compassion and imagination. Rajabali mocked Barker's example of suffering children with some bluster about the absurdity of having invincible children."

However, this interpretation overlooks the metaphorical and philosophical nature of Rajabali's argument. He was not mocking suffering children but illustrating how immunity from harm would undermine moral responsibility and the concept of moral growth.

That said, one could argue that Rajabali might have benefited from expressing more visible compassion in his rhetorical style, especially when discussing emotionally charged examples like dying children. His logical argument, while consistent and coherent, may have come across as emotionally detached to some listeners.

In summary, Carrier is correct in identifying the Trial Defense as Rajabali's strongest response to the Argument from Evil. However, his critique appears to undervalue the internal consistency and theological depth of Rajabali's framework. While valid from a secular or empirical standpoint, Carrier's insistence that the presence of evil necessarily disproves God's goodness fails to engage with the spiritual and metaphysical foundations of Rajabali's argument. Moreover, Barker's failure to adequately challenge this defense leaves the argument largely intact within the scope of the debate. Thus, while Carrier's criticisms are compelling from one paradigm, they fall short of offering a full rebuttal within the paradigm that Rajabali consistently operated from.

Shoring Up Agnosticism

Richard Carrier observed that Barker, while deploying three foundational critiques of theism—the God-of-the-Gaps fallacy, the problem of unfalsifiability, and the plausibility of naturalism—did not sufficiently develop them. Carrier also argued that Rajabali misunderstood the concept of agnosticism and failed to engage with the implications of belief in a revealed God. While Carrier raises several valid points about rhetorical strategy and missed opportunities, his assessment of Rajabali's position, particularly regarding agnosticism, is overstated and in parts misleading. This section aims to critically assess the validity of Carrier's claims against the actual debate transcript and philosophical context.

1. The "Trifecta" of Atheist Arguments: Introduced but Underdeveloped

Carrier accurately identifies that Dan Barker introduced a strategic set of arguments commonly deployed in atheistic reasoning:

That invoking God in place of scientific uncertainty constitutes a God-of-the-Gaps fallacy.

That theological claims, being unfalsifiable, are beyond meaningful verification or disproof.

That a naturalistic worldview, though incomplete, is more plausible because it relies on testable, evidence-based reasoning.

These points were clearly raised in Barker's opening and rebuttal. He argued, for instance, "Evidence of our ignorance is not evidence for God," directly addressing the gaps in knowledge often used to support religious belief. He also criticized the inability to falsify God's existence, suggesting that such claims fall outside the domain of meaningful discourse.

However, as Carrier rightly notes, these arguments were not elaborated or concretized with sufficient clarity. Barker did not tie them together as a cumulative case, nor did he illustrate them with pointed examples or apply them directly to Rajabali's specific theistic claims. For instance, while he referenced naturalism's success in explaining phenomena, he did not juxtapose it against Rajabali's cosmological or teleological claims in a structured way. As a result, while the arguments were introduced, they were not made accessible to a general audience, nor were they used to fully corner Rajabali's position.

Thus, Carrier's claim that Barker's deployment of the "trifecta" was present but underpowered is fair and constructive.

2. Was Rajabali Confused About Agnosticism?

The more contentious assertion in Carrier's analysis is that Rajabali misunderstood agnosticism and treated it as a form of indecision or ideological incoherence. According him, Rajabali "treated agnosticism as some sort of 'state of indecision,'" and criticized it unfairly for lacking ideological commitment. He says:

"Rajabali clearly didn't understand the equivalence of proper agnosticism and soft atheism, and instead treated agnosticism as some sort of 'state of indecision', thus arguing that agnosticism is not acceptable because 'You can't float forever in some limbo with no ideology.'"

This, however, does not accurately reflect the philosophical structure of Rajabali's response.

While Rajabali did critique agnosticism, his objection was not that it is illogical or academically invalid. Rather, he argued that perpetual agnosticism on fundamental existential questions is inadequate for a coherent moral or spiritual life. He stated, "You cannot float forever in some limbo with no ideology," suggesting that individuals must eventually commit to a worldview that can guide their ethical decisions, identity, and purpose.

This position echoes existentialist and theistic critiques of agnosticism that point to its pragmatic insufficiency, not its logical invalidity. Rajabali acknowledged that people may pass through phases of doubt or questioning—indeed, Islam recognizes this as a natural part of spiritual growth—but he argued that a sustained posture of epistemic indecision, especially when faced with moral responsibility, fails to provide a workable basis for human life.

Carrier's assertion that Rajabali equates agnosticism with ignorance or ideological vacuum is thus a caricature. Rajabali was responding to the popular agnostic posture often adopted in contemporary secularism, not the narrowly defined epistemic position in academic philosophy. His concern was existential: agnosticism, while logically valid, may not provide existential traction for the moral and spiritual demands of life.

3. Revealed Religion and Asymmetrical Evidence

The final claim in Carrier's critique—that Rajabali failed to address the epistemological burden created by belief in a revealed God—is more compelling.

Revealed religion, by definition, presupposes that some individuals receive direct communication or signs from God (e.g., prophets, saints), while others receive such knowledge only secondhand, through scripture or tradition. Carrier rightly notes that this raises the question: why doesn't God reveal Himself to everyone equally, especially if salvation or judgment depends on belief?

This issue was not fully addressed by Rajabali in the debate. While he defended the rationality of belief in God, and gestured toward metaphysical and moral signs, he did not fully engage with the asymmetry created by divine revelation. Barker did not press this point forcefully either, but Carrier is correct that the issue presents a strategic challenge to revealed religion, especially regarding epistemic fairness and the sufficiency of testimony.

That said, Rajabali could have drawn on Islamic resources—such as the concept of fitrah (innate disposition to know God), the idea that all people receive sufficient guidance, and that divine justice considers personal circumstances and knowledge. Still, this line of reasoning was only implicitly touched upon, not explicitly defended, which left a potential vulnerability in his apologetic position.

Conclusion: A Balanced Reassessment

Carrier's critique contains both valid insights and overstatements. On the one hand, the claim that Barker did not sufficiently develop his atheistic "trifecta" is well-taken, as is the observation that revealed religion raises unresolved epistemological challenges regarding asymmetry of evidence. On the other hand, the accusation that Rajabali fundamentally misunderstood agnosticism is philosophically unfair. Rajabali's critique was rooted not in definitional ignorance, but in an existential concern over the adequacy of agnosticism as a long-term worldview.

Ultimately, the review would have benefited from a clearer distinction between rhetorical strategy and philosophical charity. Rajabali's arguments deserve to be evaluated within the metaphysical framework from which they arise, rather than dismissed on the basis of definitional or cultural misunderstandings. While atheists may disagree with his conclusions, the debate would be better served by acknowledging the depth of his reasoning, even while scrutinizing its assumptions and implications.

Pitching Balls for the Home Team

In debates over the existence of God, audience engagement can significantly influence perceptions of who "won" the exchange. Particularly in the Q&A session, where structured arguments give way to extemporaneous responses, opportunities arise for supporters of either side to challenge, clarify, or strategically reinforce key points. In this context, Richard Carrier provided a commentary titled "Pitching Balls for the Home Team", reflecting on two questions he submitted to the panel—both of which were read by the moderator. While rhetorically sharp and strategically self-aware, Carrier's framing of Rajabali's answers warrants closer examination for accuracy and fairness. What follows evaluates whether Carrier's interpretation of Rajabali's responses to those two questions accurately represents the content and tone of the original responses, or whether it selectively simplifies them in favor of rhetorical effect.

1. The Question of Salvation: "Why Believe?"

Carrier's first question probed the ethical logic of divine justice: Why believe in God if good people who do not believe are still punished? Wouldn't a just and merciful God treat equally good individuals equally, regardless of their beliefs?[1] The concern at the heart of this question is a familiar one in religious discourse: the apparent injustice of condemning sincere non-believers to eternal punishment solely for

---

1   Refer to the third question during the Q&A exchange in the transcript.

a "lack of belief."

Carrier characterizes Rajabali's response in stark terms:

"Rajabali's answer was decidedly uncompassionate (basically, atheists deserve what they get)..."

He adds that Dan Barker seized on this response to highlight what Carrier viewed as an ethically questionable theology, one that unjustly condemns people for what may be honest disbelief. But does this summary accurately reflect Rajabali's answer?

When presented with Carrier's question, Rajabali responded by shifting focus to the metaphysical necessity of God and the moral implications of theism:

"So, do we need God? Yes. Not only for our existence, but our moral codes are derived from that too. There is a higher, longer focus for human beings, ethical standards; the deed that I do today is accountable in the hereafter."

He then elaborated on how divine accountability creates a moral framework grounded in justice, contrasting it with an atheistic worldview in which, he claimed, morality lacks binding consequences:

"As far as unbelievers, an atheist says, committing a perfect crime is a good deed—as long as you don't get caught, it's fine."

Carrier appears to have seized on this last line as evidence of an uncompassionate view of atheists, interpreting it as a blanket statement that atheists are immoral or deserving of Hell. But a closer look at Rajabali's comments—and the broader theological framework he drew from—suggests a more nuanced position.

Rajabali was not suggesting that all atheists actively commit crimes or deserve condemnation. Instead, he was critiquing the philosophical foundation of atheistic moral theory, particularly one without divine accountability. His example of the "perfect crime" was not a direct accusation, but a rhetorical illustration of the dangers of moral relativism in a worldview without God.

More importantly, Rajabali did not say that atheists "deserve what they get." Nor did he claim that mere disbelief, absent context or intention, automatically leads to eternal punishment. In fact, elsewhere in the debate, he emphasized that divine justice is individualized and based on the intention behind one's beliefs or disbelief:

"Hell is something you and I earn due to our own rejections… the Qur'anic perspective is those who go to Hell will say—it is because of our own misdeeds. Had we listened, had we obeyed, had we accepted what was given to us that was so prevalent, we would not be the inmates of this punishment…"

This statement undercuts Carrier's claim that Rajabali supported punishment merely for intellectual disagreement. Rajabali's argument aligns more closely with the traditional Islamic view: that people are judged not for ignorance or honest confusion, but for willful rejection of truth, when that truth has been clearly presented and understood.

Thus, Carrier's summary of Rajabali's response is rhetorically sharp but ultimately reductive. It fails to capture the full scope and conditionality of Rajabali's theological reasoning and overlooks his repeated insistence that God's justice is tailored to each individual's capacity, intention, and sincerity.

By flattening a deeply nuanced argument into a soundbite—"atheists deserve what they get"—Carrier diminishes both the intellectual integrity of the exchange and the complexity of Islamic moral theology. A more charitable and accurate reading would recognize that Rajabali did not condemn atheists per se, but instead challenged the coherence of moral accountability in atheism while affirming that God judges based on knowledge, sincerity, and humility—not labels.

2. Science and the Limits of Explanation: "Would You Ever Change

Your Mind?"

The question was designed, by Carrier's own admission, to "put [Rajabali's] position into sharp relief" by revealing what he interpreted as the speaker's epistemic dogmatism.[1] Carrier writes:

"I asked whether, if science one day explained everything, would he then concede that there might not be a god after all? He said this was impossible: science can never and will never explain everything, and therefore (in effect) atheism was impossible... he was basically saying he can never be wrong about God's existence."

Carrier concludes that Rajabali's response demonstrated "closed-mindedness," which he believes was made visible to all present, and subsequently exploited effectively by Dan Barker.

However, an examination of the actual exchange between Carrier and Rajabali—rooted in the transcript—reveals a far more philosophically sophisticated response than Carrier suggests. Rather than refusing to entertain the possibility of being wrong, Rajabali makes a clear distinction between scientific explanation and metaphysical grounding, anchoring his position not in dogmatism but in classical theistic reasoning.

Rajabali's Response: Science and the Limits of Explanation

In response to Carrier's question, Rajabali stated:

"You are asking a question which is really an impossibility by its own nature. If you say that there is a reasonable answer (explanation) for no creator, the reasonable answer (explanation) first of all, you have to jump over the basic hurdle of asking yourself, how does a relative universe come into existence by itself. Whatever that answer that

---

[1] In Carrier's words: "Rajabali was defending a novel form of presuppositionalism and I wanted to test it."

you're going to give me has to be God, whether you want to call it God... Supreme Power is what we are discussing."

He concluded: "The infinite power is a necessity... anything less than that is not sufficient."

Rajabali's answer is grounded in the metaphysical conviction that a contingent universe cannot account for its own existence. This argument traces its philosophical roots to thinkers such as Ibn Sīnā (Avicenna), Thomas Aquinas, and Gottfried Leibniz, who each held that contingent realities point toward a necessary being—that is, a being whose essence is existence and who is not dependent on anything else.

Rajabali is not suggesting that "science can never explain anything," nor is he rejecting empirical inquiry. Rather, he insists that science operates within a metaphysical framework that it does not and cannot explain. His point is that no amount of scientific explanation can eliminate the need for metaphysical grounding. Even if science could describe the mechanism behind the universe's origin, the fundamental question of why there is something rather than nothing would remain.

Framing the Question: Reductionism vs. Philosophical Realism

Carrier's question assumes that science might one day explain "everything", and that such a total explanatory power might render God unnecessary. Rajabali counters by highlighting that science, by definition, cannot transcend its own domain: it deals with empirical, observable, relative phenomena, not with absolute, necessary being.

In Rajabali's words, "the relative universe"—that is, a universe of dependent, mutable entities—cannot explain itself. Even if science could trace back every event and structure to a singularity or precondition, the fact that those structures require explanation persists. His response is not one of epistemic stubbornness but of metaphysical realism. He is saying, in effect: whatever ultimate explanation you offer must necessarily fulfill the criteria of God—self-existent, necessary, and foundational.

This is not a refusal to consider evidence or reason. Rather, Rajabali is arguing that rational inquiry inevitably points to a necessary cause, whether one calls it "God," "Supreme Power," or "necessary being." He leaves the label open but insists on the philosophical necessity of such a foundation. This is in line with a long tradition of contingency arguments, not an evasion of evidence.

Is This "Closed-Mindedness"?

Carrier characterizes Rajabali's philosophical commitment as epistemic inflexibility, even going so far as to say:

"He was basically saying he can never be wrong about God's existence."

This is a mischaracterization. Rajabali is not claiming infallibility in the sense of personal certainty immune to evidence; rather, he is asserting that the structure of reality—as it is currently understood and experienced—requires a transcendent, necessary ground. Unless a challenger can philosophically demonstrate how contingent beings can exist without a cause, Rajabali's position remains rationally and metaphysically justified.

Moreover, Rajabali's openness to discussing the definition of God—as "whatever you want to call it"—indicates a level of conceptual flexibility. He is not rigidly attached to a theistic model based on revealed scripture in this specific argument but is making a broader metaphysical point about necessity vs. contingency.

Did Barker Seize the Opportunity?

Carrier commends Dan Barker for capitalizing on Rajabali's answer. It is true that Barker reiterated the idea that theism often invokes unfalsifiable claims, and that framing Rajabali's position as unassailable might make it look immune to critique. However, Barker did not directly challenge the metaphysical structure of Rajabali's answer.

He did not provide an alternative account of contingency, nor did he dispute the necessity of grounding being in an absolute cause.

Thus, while Barker may have scored rhetorical points by framing the theist as dogmatic, he left Rajabali's philosophical reasoning largely unaddressed.

Conclusion: Certainty Grounded in Reason

Rajabali's answer was not an admission of blind faith, but a philosophical commitment to the necessity of a foundational cause. His view is not "closed-minded" in the sense of refusing to engage with contrary evidence; it is a reflection of a deep metaphysical conviction grounded in centuries of philosophical thought.

Carrier's characterization, while rhetorically sharp, fails to appreciate the philosophical depth of Rajabali's position. It conflates metaphysical certainty with intellectual dogmatism, and in doing so, misrepresents a key part of the debate.

Far from refusing to think, Rajabali invites us to think more deeply—about what explanations count, and what reality ultimately requires.

Epilogue

Throughout this book, we have traced the contours of a remarkable debate—one that unfolded not only on a public stage in post-9/11 New York, but within the minds and convictions of those present, and those who continue to engage with the timeless question: Does God not exist?

This unusual framing—flipping the more common proposition "Does God exist?"—subtly shifted the burden of proof. It was now the atheist, Dan Barker, who had to demonstrate the impossibility or improbability of God's existence. Yet what emerged was more than a contest over philosophical territory. It became a conversation between two entire worldviews—one grounded in empirical skepticism and secular humanism, and the other in transcendent metaphysics and divine-centered purpose.

At the heart of this exchange stood a concept that perhaps proved more formidable than either debater expected: the problem of frame of reference in proving or disproving God's existence.

The Frame of Reference Dilemma:

Hassanain Rajabali repeatedly insisted that God cannot be meaningfully proven or disproven within the narrow confines of the human frame of reference, because God transcends all the conditions that define that frame. Time, space, causality, even thought itself—all are, in the theistic view, contingent features of creation. God, as the Absolute Being, is not in time or bound by space. He is not an object within the universe that can be measured or observed. He is the cause of causes, the source of being, the necessary existent (*wājib al-wujūd*) upon which all relative and contingent things depend.

To attempt to prove God by dragging Him into the empirical frame,

Rajabali argued, is to misunderstand what the word 'God' even means. Worse, it risks reducing the Absolute to the relative—treating the Infinite as if it were finite. The result, he warned, is incoherence or misrepresentation.

This was a key moment in the debate. For here Rajabali was not merely offering a theological doctrine, but a philosophical challenge: how can finite creatures, bound by time and sensory experience, meaningfully speak of—or reason toward—an infinite, eternal, and transcendent Being?

The Human Desire for Comprehensibility:

Dan Barker, in response, took a predictable and intellectually honest path. He resisted the move to transcendence as, in his view, a way of placing God beyond scrutiny. He asserted that any meaningful concept of God must be coherent, definable, and, at least in principle, falsifiable. If a being cannot be tested, experienced, or rationally differentiated from "nothing," then the proposition of such a being's existence becomes empty.

For Barker, to describe God as a "blob of infinite unknowability" is to describe Him out of existence—not disprove Him, but to demonstrate that the concept itself fails the test of intelligibility. And indeed, from a purely empirical framework, this is not an unreasonable position.

But what Barker perhaps failed to fully grasp—at least within the context of Islamic theology and metaphysical reasoning—is that the problem of incomprehensibility is not a bug, but a feature. The divine, by definition, must lie beyond the realm of full comprehension. Not because God is obscure, but because our tools for knowing are limited. We cannot wrap our minds around infinity, not because infinity is illogical, but because we are finite.

Indirect Knowledge and Traces of the Divine:

Rajabali's argument, though not always formally structured, echoed a rich tradition in Islamic and classical theistic thought: that we come to know the existence of God not by direct perception, but by observing the marks He leaves in His creation. This is sometimes referred to as sign-based knowledge (*'ilm bi al-āthār*)—the idea that creation bears the fingerprints of the Creator.

Order, beauty, consciousness, rationality, morality—these are not mere accidents or illusions. They are signs (*āyāt*) pointing to something beyond themselves. In Rajabali's view, the universe is not neutral—it is intelligible, and that intelligibility invites the human mind to ask the question: Why is there something rather than nothing? And more than that: Why does this "something" function so precisely, so purposefully, so finely tuned to allow life, consciousness, and meaning?

To this, Rajabali argued, theism offers the most coherent answer: not only does God exist, but His existence makes sense of ours.

God and the Limits of Proof:

But even so, we return to the tension that haunts every debate of this nature: Can God be proven? And if not, does that mean belief is irrational?

Here, the discussion enters deeper waters. For what is a "proof"? Is it logical necessity? Scientific demonstration? Existential conviction? Religious experience?

Rajabali's position implies that expecting "proof" of God in the same sense that we prove mathematical equations or conduct scientific experiments is a category error. God is not a scientific hypothesis. He is not an object in the sky or a mechanism in the genome. He is Being itself—the foundation for all reality. And foundational truths are not always directly "provable." We do not prove the law of non-contradiction or the existence of consciousness—we start with them.

Likewise, the argument goes, God is not proven in a lab, but recognized through reason, through reflection, and through what the Qur'an calls *tafakkur*—the contemplative process by which the human being reads the signs of the universe and uncovers their ultimate ground.

Faith as Recognition, Not Blindness:

From this vantage, faith is not the enemy of reason, but its continuation. It is not a leap into darkness, but a response to what one perceives—dimly perhaps, but unmistakably—in the light of reflection. It is, as Rajabali implied, not believing in spite of the evidence, but because of it—because the universe calls out for an explanation, and nothing within it can explain itself.

Dan Barker's insistence on empirical verification serves an important purpose. It guards against delusion and warns against uncritical belief. But it also risks closing the door to forms of knowledge that do not fit into the empirical mold, including moral intuition, aesthetic experience, metaphysical reasoning, and the ineffable sense of the sacred.

The Final Question:

In the end, the question "Does God not exist?" cannot be answered by a syllogism alone. It must be approached through multiple levels of knowing—logical, existential, moral, spiritual.

The debate between Rajabali and Barker highlighted this fact: they were not merely exchanging arguments; they were inhabiting different worlds of thought. Barker spoke from within a world framed by the observable and the provable. Rajabali spoke from a world where the observable leads to the unobservable, and where reason, though necessary, is ultimately fulfilled only when it bows in humility before that which exceeds it.

This book has sought not to crown a victor, but to enrich the reader's understanding of the terrain. Whether you find yourself leaning toward skepticism or belief, what matters most is that the question continues to live in you—not as a burden, but as a call.

For perhaps, in the end, the search for God is not about arriving at a final proof, but about asking the only question worthy of a human being: What is the source of all that is? And what does it mean to live in response to that source?

That question remains. And so does the journey for the seekers of truth!

www.ingramcontent.com/pod-product-compliance
Lightning Source LLC
Chambersburg PA
CBHW031250290426
44109CB00012B/510